Great Quarterbacks of the NFL

Colorful profiles of ten famous NFL quarterbacks, with gripping accounts of the big games in which they starred. The big ten include Johnny Unitas, Sammy Baugh, Sid Luckman, Y. A. Tittle, Otto Graham, Norm Van Brocklin, Frank Ryan, Bart Starr, Fran Tarkenton and Charley Johnson.

RANDOM HOUSE   NEW YORK

Great Quarterbacks of the NFL

BY DAVE ANDERSON

ILLUSTRATED WITH PHOTOGRAPHS

Library of Congress Catalog Card Number: 65–22658
Designed by Peter Schaefer
Manufactured in the United States of America

Photograph credits: Vernon J. Biever, vi, 40, 65, 74, 93, 130, 136, 138, 147, 149, 172–175; Columbia University Dept. of Sports Information, 50; New York *Daily News*, 111; United Press International, title page, 5, 18, 20, 23, 25, 45, 55, 59, 70–71, 76, 83, 85, 96, 103, 108, 128, 144, 164; Herb Weitman, 168; Wide World, 9, 30, 33, 89, 105, 119, 126, 156, 161.

Cover: Walter Iooss, Jr.

Contents

Introduction

Quarterback is a unique position in pro football. No other position demands such a burden of responsibility.

The quarterback's teammates only have to think for themselves. Block the linebacker. Run the down-and-out pass pattern. Take the handoff and slant off-tackle. But the quarterback must think for everybody. In the huddle he calls the play. But when he hunches over the center, he must check the opposing defense and often he must change the play. In a matter of seconds he decides on a new play and transmits it by verbal code to his teammates.

If the play is a run, the quarterback must execute the handoff or pitch-out perfectly. If it is a pass, he must choose his target almost instantaneously. And he must hit that target consistently. Hit or miss, he often must drag himself off the ground after being flattened by clawing opponents.

The good quarterback must survive this mental and physical punishment play after play throughout the season. To be a great one, he must not only survive, he must win. Of all the quarterbacks in the National Football League, only one emerges

each season as the quarterback of the championship team. Over the seasons only a few have
emerged as *great* quarterbacks.

The quarterbacks included in this book are considered to be *great* quarterbacks. The list includes
such old timers as Sammy Baugh, Sid Luckman,
Otto Graham, Norm Van Brocklin and the recently retired Y. A. Tittle. Johnny Unitas has
been stamped as a *great* quarterback, too. And the
four others included were still earning the *great*
label in the 1964 season. They are Bart Starr, Fran
Tarkenton, Frank Ryan and Charley Johnson.

It takes an extraordinary collection of talents to
develop into a *great* quarterback. A good passing
arm, for example, is merely a starter. The quarterback needs much more.

He must have the courage to defy the pass
rushers who surround him as he waits, apparently
so nonchalantly, until the last split second before
releasing his pass. He must have the intelligence
to call the correct play at the correct time. And he
must have leadership. His teammates must respect
him and look to him in moments of despair.

The quarterback has been described as meaning
"everything" to a team's offense. The quarterbacks
in this volume have meant nearly everything not
only to their teams, but also to the success of the
National Football League.

Great Quarterbacks of the NFL

Johnny Unitas

1

The Baltimore Colts were losing, 17–14, to the New York Giants. In the dusk at Yankee Stadium, the scoreboard clock blinked *1:56*—one minute and fifty-six seconds to play. Not much time. Perhaps not enough time. The Colts had the ball on their own 14-yard line after forcing the Giants to punt. But now, in this 1958 National Football League (NFL) championship game, they had to get close enough to kick a tying field goal. If they could accomplish this, the game would go to overtime. As the Colt offense trotted onto the field, quarterback Johnny Unitas buckled the chin strap on his white helmet and hunched into the huddle.

"Now," he said, "we're going to find out what

we're made of. Unless the clock is stopped, we won't have time for any more huddles. Stay alert. I'll call the plays at the line of scrimmage."

Unitas hit Lenny Moore with a pass for an 11-yard gain and a first down. The Colts lined up quickly and Unitas, cool as ice, completed another pass, this time to end Raymond Berry. It was a 25-yard gain to midfield. The Colts lined up again without a huddle and Unitas barked the signals. Another pass to Berry for a 15-yard gain to the Giant 35-yard line. Again Unitas passed to Berry, this time for a 22-yard gain to the Giant 13. The clock was ticking off the final seconds as the Colt place-kicking specialist, Steve Myrha, ran onto the field.

At the 20-yard line Myrha swung his foot and the ball sailed through the goal posts for a field goal, tying the game, 17–17. The scoreboard clock showed seven seconds to play.

Until this 1958 game, the NFL had never had a tie in one of its championships. But in anticipation of such an event the League had recently agreed to a "sudden-death" provision. In case of a tie, the game would continue with further 15-minute quarters, ending when one team made a score of any kind.

Johnny Unitas

The Colts had been successful in creating a "sudden-death" situation. They still had a chance. Their defensive unit forced the Giants to punt. Then Johnny Unitas took over. The Colts, starting from their own 20-yard line, marched deep into Giant territory. With a second down on the Giant eight-yard line, Unitas called a daring play: a sideline pass to tight end Jim Mutscheller. Had one of the Giant defensive backs intercepted, the New Yorker would have had a clear field and a touchdown. But Unitas hit Mutscheller at the Giant one-yard line. On the third down Unitas spun and handed off to fullback Alan "The Horse" Ameche, who rammed through the Giant line into the end zone. The Colts had won, 23–17, and fans still call the 1958 NFL playoff the "greatest game" in football history.

A few minutes later, Johnny Unitas, the player most responsible for its being the greatest game, leaned against his locker.

His white jersey with the big blue "19" was streaked with dirt and grass stains. So were his gray pants. But Johnny Unitas was smiling as he spoke to the crowd of newsmen jammed around him.

"That pass to Mutscheller on second down," one of the newsmen asked, "weren't you taking a risk there on an interception?"

Unitas grinned. "When you know what you're doing," he answered, "you don't get intercepted. I knew the play would work."

In those few words Johnny Unitas showed what has made him a top-ranking quarterback. He is a daredevil. But more than that, he possesses the confidence of a successful daredevil, not the recklessness of a losing daredevil. Behind it all, of course, is his ability. He can throw the long pass or the short one. He handles the ball. He runs when he has to. He calls the proper plays. He even blocks occasionally, which is unusual for a quarterback. Equally important, he commands respect from his teammates and he's physically tough. He plays despite injuries.

During the 1958 season, for example, Unitas suffered three cracked ribs and a collapsed lung in a game with the Green Bay Packers. Three weeks later, after missing only two games, he played with a heavy harness protecting the damaged area. On his first play, he hit Lenny Moore with a 58-yard touchdown pass.

In 1960 he played despite a painful back injury that bothered him throughout the season. In 1961 he dislocated the middle finger on his throwing hand early in the season. The finger hindered his passing during the remainder of the year, but he suffered silently. He was following the creed of all

NFL competitors: to play if at all possible.

One day in 1960 he lived up to this creed as few players have. His back injury ached. To make it worse the Chicago Bears were winning, 20–17, in the final minute. The Colts had fourth down on the Bear 39-yard line. Unitas was groggy. He had been buried by the Bear pass rushers on the second down, and again on the third down. Both times the Colt trainer had rushed out to assist him to his feet.

"C'mon, John," one of his teammates said, "get out of here. You're asking for a real serious injury."

"It's only one more play," Unitas said, wincing. "I can throw one more. Don't worry, I'll be all right."

At the snap Unitas faded back and, despite his aching and sore body, fired a pass to Lenny Moore for the winning touchdown.

Moments such as this have earned Johnny Unitas acclaim as the best quarterback in football. The record book supports his reputation. During one great playing streak, he threw at least one touchdown pass in every one of forty-seven consecutive games. This is a record on a par with Joe DiMaggio's famous 56-game hitting streak in baseball. In the future, Unitas—barring injury— should break all NFL passing records for completions, yardage and touchdowns. But just as he

8

Johnny Unitas

proved himself as a great quarterback in winning the 1958 and 1959 championship games, he proved himself as a great human being after losing one, 27–0, to the Cleveland Browns in 1964. In the dressing room that day he told newsmen:

Johnny Unitas on December 27, 1964—the day he couldn't lead the Colts to a championship.

"No excuses. They just beat us bad. And would you fellows do me a favor? When you go into the Browns' dressing room, tell Frank Ryan 'Congratulations' for me. I thought he quarterbacked a great game for them."

Johnny Unitas is always thinking of the other person, whether it is an opponent or a teammate. One evening during the 1964 season he and Alex Sandusky, the right guard of the Colts, were having dinner with their wives in a suburban Baltimore restaurant. They had finished their steaks when a small boy, holding an autograph book and a pen, stopped at the table.

"May I have your autograph, Mister Unitas?" the boy asked.

John wrote his name and handed the book back to the boy. Not recognizing Alex Sandusky, the young fan was about to walk away. This is not unusual. Guards toil anonymously. They usually are appreciated only by their teammates. But Johnny Unitas had special reason to appreciate Alex Sandusky. For years the husky guard's blocking had protected him. In the split second before the small boy walked away, Unitas said:

"This is Alex Sandusky, son. Get his autograph, too."

Such unselfishness comes naturally to Johnny Unitas. When the Colts won the 1958 NFL title, for example, a man from the Ed Sullivan television show rushed up to him in the Colt locker room.

"John," he said, "we want you to take a bow on tonight's show. We'll pay you $750."

Unitas thought for a moment. No question but what $750 was a fat fee for merely taking a bow on television. But the rest of the team was returning immediately to Baltimore. To go on the Sullivan show, he would have to remain in New York.

"Thanks," Johnny said, "but I'm staying with the players."

"What for?" the television man said. "You've won the championship. You don't *have* to go back to Baltimore now."

"I know," Johnny said, "but being with the players tonight is more important to me than $750."

John Constantine Unitas had come a long way. Until he clicked with the Colts, he had always been the quarterback nobody wanted. The Colts, in fact, signed him for just the price of a long-distance phone call to his Pittsburgh home. Nowadays college quarterbacks sign pro contracts for hundreds of thousands of dollars. But the best of today's professional quarterbacks, Johnny Unitas, signed merely for the opportunity to make the team. He had always wanted to play pro football

—so much so that a few weeks before the Colts called him, he had been playing semipro football for six dollars a game. Within ten years, he was playing for a salary of more than $60,000 a season. But his rise to fame and fortune did not spoil him.

Born on May 7, 1933, in Pittsburgh, he was often disappointed, but never discouraged. "I'll never be oversatisfied about anything," he once said, "because all I have to do is think of my mother's situation after my father died."

There were four Unitas children, the oldest only ten. Their mother kept their father's coal-trucking business going for a few months after his death. She also worked at night, scrubbing floors in downtown Pittsburgh office buildings. Later she worked in a bakery and sold insurance while studying bookkeeping at night.

"When she took her civil-service exam," John says proudly, "she got the highest mark in the class." She became a bookkeeper for the city of Pittsburgh. "My mother never really liked football," John says, "but she taught me more about it, by her example of what it takes to get ahead, than any of my coaches. And I've had some good coaches."

At St. Justin's High School, Unitas was the All-Catholic quarterback in the Pittsburgh area. But at that time he was a skinny schoolboy who weighed just 145 pounds. His mother couldn't afford to send him to college; he had to get an athletic scholarship. One of his teachers, the Reverend Thomas J. McCarthy, arranged for a tryout at Notre Dame.

Two weeks later a letter from Notre Dame arrived. But when John opened it, he read the words he had feared: too small.

Indiana University turned him down, too. So did Maryland and Lehigh. Finally, desperate to play football, he attended a tryout at the University of Louisville.

"You can throw the ball," the coach, Frank Camp, told him. "And you'll put on a few pounds. You got yourself a free ride."

Johnny Unitas had his athletic scholarship: tuition, board, room, books, fees and $25 a month for laundry and incidentals.

At the time Louisville was not a member of the National Collegiate Athletic Association, so freshmen there were eligible for varsity competition. Midway through his freshman season in 1951, Unitas got a chance to play in a game against St. Bonaventure's. He threw for three touchdowns and his passes gained more than 300 yards. He was on his way to stardom. By the end of his senior season, his four-year record was 245 completions in 502 passes for 2,912 yards and 27 touchdowns. As Coach Camp had predicted, he had filled out physically, too. He was six-feet-one and weighed 195 pounds.

One day a Cleveland Browns scout stopped by the Louisville campus. "We might take you as a late-round choice in the draft," he told Unitas. By draft, he meant the National Football League's annual selection of graduating college gridiron stars.

But on the day of the NFL draft, his hometown Pittsburgh Steelers selected Johnny Unitas in the eighth round. He was elated. Now he would have a chance to play pro football in his own backyard. In July, 1955, he reported to the Steeler training camp at Olean, New York. He passed the ball well in the workouts, but there were three other quarterbacks ahead of him—Jim Finks, Ted Marchibroda and Vic Eaton. The Steeler coach, Walt Kiesling, didn't use Unitas in any of the pre-season games. Shortly before the Steelers were to break camp, Unitas was told to report to Kiesling's office.

"Son," the coach said, "we're going to have to release you. But here's ten dollars to get you home to Pittsburgh."

Unitas took the money and walked out of Kiesling's office. He went to his dormitory room and packed his bag. Soon he was on his way into town to catch a bus for Pittsburgh.

"Unitas is gone, eh?" Finks asked a teammate that day. "That's lucky for me. He was the best passer here."

Unitas, disappointed but not discouraged, was hoping to catch on with another NFL team. The Browns, who had planned to draft him, were having quarterback problems. Unitas wired Coach Paul Brown, asking for a chance. But unknown to Unitas, Brown had talked veteran Otto Graham into coming out of retirement for another season. Nevertheless, Brown answered with an encouraging telegram:

"No need for you this season. Suggest you come to camp next summer for tryout. Contact me in the spring."

So for the 1955 season Johnny Unitas worked on a pile-driver. He needed the money. He had married his high-school sweetheart, Dorothy Hoelle, and they were expecting their first child. But he still wanted to play pro football. And because he knew he had to stay in top form for the Browns' training camp the following summer, he joined the Bloomfield Rams, a semipro team, at six dollars a game.

Then, one day in February of 1956, his phone rang.

"This is Don Kellett, the general manager of the Baltimore Colts," the voice said. "We've just claimed you from the Steelers."

The Colts were short on quarterbacks. They had an experienced starter in George Shaw. But their second stringer, Gary Kerkorian, had retired from football to go to law school.

"We'd like to get a look at you," Kellett said. "We're having a tryout camp in May. We'd like you to come down to it and work out."

At the May camp, Unitas impressed Colt Coach Wilbur (Weeb) Ewbank.

Soon after the young quarterback returned to Pittsburgh, a steel strike ended his job. In a way it was a break, for in the weeks before the Colt training camp opened, he worked to get into top physical shape. He also practiced his passing. "My coach at Louisville, Frank Camp, got me in the habit of practicing thirty to forty-five minutes a day," Unitas has said. "Specialists can never practice their specialties too much. The danger is not practicing enough. Make that mistake and soon you may not be a specialist any more."

Unitas made the Colts as the second stringer behind Shaw. Then, in an early-season game at Chicago, Shaw suffered a knee injury.

"All right, John," Ewbank told him on the sideline, "just go in there and do your best. You've wanted this chance. Here it is."

The Colts were leading, 21–20, when Unitas took over. But he could not have done worse. He fumbled three handoffs and the Bears turned each one into a touchdown. He overthrew a receiver and the Bears intercepted and ran it back for another touchdown. The Bears won, 58–27. To make things worse for Unitas, the Colts asked Gary Kerkorian to return to the team while Shaw was injured. But Kerkorian needed time to get in shape. Until he was ready, the Colts had to continue to use rookie quarterback Johnny Unitas. It was all the time he needed.

In the next game he threw two touchdown passes against the Green Bay Packers. Then the Colts routed the Los Angeles Rams, 56–21, and Unitas clinched a job. When the 1957 season started, he was the number one quarterback. The Colts finished in third place in the Western Division. In 1958 and 1959 they won the NFL championship. Suddenly John Unitas was Mister Quarterback. Then, throughout the next few seasons, he was haunted by injuries. And just as Unitas was given credit for the good seasons, he was blamed for the bad ones.

He was booed by the Baltimore fans, notorious for their cruelty. He took it calmly, but the booing left a psychological scar.

"Mr. Quarterback" breaks through the Giants' line, gaining 16 yards for the Colts in the second quarter of the 1959 championship game.

One day during the 1964 season, while the Colts were in the midst of their 11-game winning streak, Unitas was cheered when he got up to speak at a luncheon.

"Well, well," he said. "It looks like we're going to have to get a bigger bandwagon for everybody to jump on these days."

The crowd buzzed. Johnny Unitas had stung them with a quick pass, so to speak, as he has stung so many NFL rivals over the years. His sharp verbal pass was nothing new. He had always had the ability to squash a loud mouth—either on or off the field. Once, when he was at the University of Louisville, he was in a fourth-down-and-two-yards-to-go situation on the opposing team's 40-yard line.

"Give me the ball. I'll get the two yards for you," the Louisville fullback suggested.

"When I want you to take it," Unitas snapped back. "I'll tell you." He called a pass. And he completed it for a touchdown as his receiver got behind the surprised defense.

Another time he was on his own two-yard line. On third down he called for a surprise pass. As he faded back into the end zone, the Louisville fans were shocked. So was his coach. But one of the Louisville receivers broke clear and Unitas hit him on the 40-yard line. The receiver ran the rest of the way for a touchdown.

Despite such daredevil heroics, Johnny Unitas was for years the quarterback nobody wanted.

Now, ironically, he is the quarterback *everybody* wants. Late in the 1964 season, he was named the NFL Player of the Year by both Associated Press and United Press International, the two major wire services. Informed of the honors, he reacted typically. "I couldn't accept these awards," he said, "without accepting them for the whole team. Without the thirty-nine other guys, I'm nothing."

Unitas proudly displays the trophy he received as the most valuable player in the 1964 All Star Pro Bowl.

But throughout the NFL almost everybody will tell you that without Johnny Unitas, the thirty-nine other guys wouldn't do so well, either.

Sammy Baugh
2

Inside D. C. Stadium the Washington Redskins were running through plays during a 1963 mid-week practice session. The stands were empty except for a tall Texan who was quietly watching the drill. Sam Baugh had last played for the Redskins in 1952, but he was back at the nation's capital to receive the first annual Sam Baugh Award. The award was to be presented each year to a past or present Redskin hero. Noticing Baugh, Redskin Coach Bill McPeak sent an aide to invite him onto the field.

"Gentlemen," McPeak said to his assembled players, "I want you to meet Sam Baugh—the greatest player the Redskins ever had."

The players, some of whom had not been born when Baugh was a rookie in 1937, broke out in a burst of applause. They had read and heard about Slingin' Sammy Baugh, perhaps the best passer in football history.

"Maybe," McPeak said, "Sam will bring us some luck."

"About all I can do for you fellows," Baugh told the players, "is get you out of the last couple minutes of practice."

"You win," McPeak said with a laugh. "Practice is over."

Sam Baugh always knew how to win. He was the first quarterback elected to the National Pro Football Hall of Fame. He led the Redskins to two National Football League championships and five Eastern Division titles.

Sam's famous rival, Sid Luckman of the Chicago Bears, once said, "Every time Sam throws a pass I learn something. Nobody is ever going to equal him." When, for the last time, Baugh took off his burgundy-and-gold Redskin jersey with the big "33," he held 16 NFL passing records and three punting records. His 16 seasons of playing with the pros established another record, too. His durability was amazing for a slim, six-feet-two 180-pounder surrounded by monster pass rushers. But he possessed the whipcord strength of a Western gun-fighter.

He possessed something else, too: a weapon as good as a gun for keeping pass rushers honest.

One day early in his Redskin career he was slammed to the ground by an opposing tackle with a tough-guy reputation. In the pileup the hatchet-man whacked Baugh across the face with his fore-arm.

"Cut it out," Sam growled.

On the next play the tackle dug one of his elbows into Baugh's mouth. Somehow the game

Sammy Baugh eluding his tacklers.

officials didn't see the fouls, but the other Redskins did.

"I'll take care of him for you," said Turk Edwards, the big Redskin captain. "I'll get him this play."

"Never mind," Baugh drawled. "I'll take care of him myself. Don't anybody try to block him this play."

Again Baugh faded back to pass. The tackle roared through to pounce on him. Sam stood there, his arm cocked, watching the tackle come closer . . . closer . . . Then Baugh fired one of his bullet passes. In those days players didn't wear face masks. The pass hit the tackle between the eyes. He went down as if he had been shot. By the time he came to, he was lying on a stretcher on the sidelines.

Word spread quickly throughout the NFL: Leave Sammy Baugh alone. His bullet passes were equally accurate at 15 yards or 50 yards. He had full confidence in their accuracy, too.

The first day that Baugh reported to the Redskin training camp, Coach Ray Flaherty stood at a blackboard diagraming the team's plays for the rookie passer. "On this one, Sam," Flaherty said, his chalk scratching across the slate, "the right end takes ten steps straight ahead, turns and comes back in a buttonhook pattern. I want you to hit him with the football right in the eye. Is that clear?"

"One question, Coach," Baugh said.

"Yes?"

"Which eye?"

Baugh's confidence in his own ability rubbed off on his teammates. Once, later in his career, the Redskins were on an opponent's two-yard line. Baugh handed off to Ed Quirk, a rookie fullback. Quirk fumbled but one of the Redskin linemen recovered.

"Quirk," Baugh barked in the huddle, "same play."

The famous Redskin quarterback in action.

"Not me, Sam," Quirk said. "I might fumble again."

"You're gonna get it till you learn to hold it."

At the snap Baugh spun and stuffed the ball into Quirk's belly. The rookie plunged into the end zone for a touchdown.

"And you know," Sam said proudly one day many years later, "Quirk hardly ever fumbled again."

Baugh was able to realize the limitations of his teammates, however. For a quarterback, this is just as important as knowing a player's potential. Once, during a blackboard session, Sam argued that a play would not work the way it was diagramed.

"Why won't it work?" the coach asked.

"Because," Sam said, "you have the halfback blocking that tackle. On Sunday that tackle isn't going to be a chalk mark. It's going to be Kilroy." Baugh was referring to Frank "Bucko" Kilroy of the Philadelphia Eagles, then the most feared tackle in the NFL. "No halfback is gonna block Kilroy," Baugh said.

"You're right, Sam," the coach agreed.

The play was changed.

Sam Baugh was a football genius, but several times his talent was nearly sidetracked.

Sammy Baugh

Born on March 17, 1914, in Temple, Texas, Samuel Adrian Baugh was the son of a Santa Fe railroad man. As a youngster he began his football career catching passes instead of throwing them. When he was 16, his family moved to Sweetwater, Texas, where he tried out for the Sweetwater High School team as an end. He made it. But one day during practice, when Baugh was running a pass pattern, the team's passer threw wildly. Sam retrieved the ball and fired it back—40 yards on a line.

"Hey, Baugh," his coach yelled, "do that again."

Sam picked up another ball and hurled it 50 yards. The coach shook his head.

"You," he said to Baugh, "are now our new passer."

Although he was a sensational schoolboy passer, he was too skinny to impress the college scouts. Not that he really cared. At the time Sam Baugh was more interested in baseball. He was rated the best teen-age third baseman in western Texas. Leo "Dutch" Meyer, the baseball coach at Texas Christian University in Fort Worth, arranged for him to attend TCU on a baseball scholarship.

"This kid Baugh plays football, too," Meyer told varsity football coach Francis Schmidt. "Maybe he'll make your team."

27

"Not a chance," Schmidt replied. "He's not big enough. He'd be broken in half in the first contact scrimmage. Too skinny."

But Meyer, the freshman football coach, liked the way Baugh threw a pass. The next season, Schmidt retired and Meyer took over as varsity football coach. Sam Baugh moved up with him. The Southwest Conference was made for Sam Baugh. In the mid-30s the razzle-dazzle passing game was new. And the fans loved it. The player they loved most was Slingin' Sammy Baugh.

As a junior he led the Horned Frogs to a 3–2 victory over Louisiana State in the Sugar Bowl—not so much with his passing as with his punting. His slender right leg could boom a ball 50 yards.

As a senior he led TCU to a Cotton Bowl victory, 16–6, over Marquette. Earlier that season he had two great days. His passes and punts upset Santa Clara. And he almost single-handedly defeated rival Texas University. In that game the TCU center, Ki Aldrich (later a Redskin teammate) taunted the Texas players.

"Attention," Aldrich announced as he was about to snap the ball. "Mister Baugh is going to pass again. I can't tell you where, but I would suggest that you be ready."

The tip-off didn't help the Texas pass defenders. Sam Baugh kept hitting his receivers time after time. But his slender physique made most of the pro scouts wary of recommending Sam. Seven teams ignored him in the NFL draft before the Redskins named him as their number one choice. But Baugh had been offered a major-league baseball contract by the St. Louis Cardinals. So George Preston Marshall, the Redskin owner, who had a reputation as a conservative spender, was forced to go higher than he ever had for a rookie.

"Sam," Marshall said. "I'll give you five thousand dollars to play for us next season. Plus a five-hundred-dollar bonus. You'll be the highest paid player on the team."

By today's standards, the money he was offered would be an insult. But then, in the midst of the Depression, it was a record amount. Baugh signed. To show him off, Marshall arranged for Baugh to come to Washington to meet the local sportswriters. Marshall was a showman. "Before you leave Texas," he told Baugh, "get yourself a ten-gallon hat and a pair of cowboy boots. I want you to be wearing them when you get off the plane."

"I never wore stuff like that," Baugh protested. "I'm no cowboy. I grew up in a town."

"You're a cowboy now," Marshall said. "I want everybody to think you just got off a horse."

"All right, Mister Marshall," Baugh said. "I'll have the outfit on. And I'll bring you the bill."

When Baugh arrived at the Washington airport, he hobbled down the ramp from the plane's exit door.

"What's the matter, Sam?" Marshall asked.

"My feet hurt. These boots pinch somethin' awful, Mister Marshall."

George Marshall greets Sammy Baugh as he arrives in Washington in his ten-gallon hat.

"You'll get used to them," Marshall said.

The Redskin coach, Ray Flaherty, was interested in Baugh's arm, not in his cowboy clothes. Flaherty arranged a private workout to inspect the rookie. Baugh fired pass after pass on target.

"George, you did it," Flaherty said to Marshall. "That's the best passer in football. We can win the championship with him."

The Redskins, while playing for Boston, had lost the 1936 championship playoff to the Green Bay Packers. Then, because interest in the team was so poor in Boston, Marshall moved the franchise to Washington. The Redskins played there for the first time during Baugh's rookie season. Before the opening game of that 1937 season, Flaherty walked to the center of the dressing room.

"At Boston," the coach told his players, "we had a good team but you men always complained that we didn't have a passer. Now we've got the best passer in the world. He'll take you to the championship."

Sam Baugh did just that. Operating as a single wing tailback, he passed the Redskins to the Eastern Division title. This earned them a crack at the Chicago Bears in the playoff for the NFL championship. In those days football was played more cautiously than it is now. It was against all strategy to pass deep in your own territory. The first time the Redskins got the ball, they were on their own nine-yard line. The field was icy. The strategy was obvious: punt out of danger.

"We're gonna go into punt formation," Baugh said in the huddle, "but we're really gonna pass. Stay awake."

Baugh waited in the end zone in punt formation. Instead, he threw a pass—perhaps the first pass ever thrown from a team's end zone in pro football history. The Bears were fooled. Cliff Battles, the Redskin fullback, was wide open. He caught the ball for a 42-yard gain. Baugh's passes kept the Redskins on the march and Battles scored from the seven-yard line on a reverse.

The Bears never recovered. Baugh threw three touchdown passes and the Redskins were the world champions, 28–21. The rookie quarterback from TCU had accomplished what Coach Ray Flaherty predicted he would.

In 1940 the Redskins again played the Bears for the championship. This time the Bears won by the classic 73–0 score. But the Redskin rooters in old Griffith Stadium in Washington believed that the Redskins might have had a chance if right end Charley Malone had not missed a touchdown pass. The Bears were ahead by only 7–0 when Malone broke free in the end zone. But he lost Baugh's pass in the glare of the sunlight. The ball hit him in the chest and fell to the ground. The Redskins never had a chance after that.

In the dressing room after the game, a newsman asked Baugh: "Suppose Malone had caught the ball? Would that have changed the game?"

"It might have," Baugh agreed with a smile. "It might have made it 73–7."

In 1942 the Redskins won their third Eastern title behind Baugh. But the Bears swept through the Western Division with an undefeated record.

Intercepting a pass in his own end zone, Baugh breaks up a scoring threat during the 1942 title game with the Bears.

This time the playoff game was in Chicago. The Bears were a big favorite. They took a quick 6–0 lead. Then Baugh zipped a 32-yard touchdown pass to Wilbur Moore, and the Bears geared their defense for passes.

"They think we're gonna pass," Baugh said in the huddle at one point, "but we're gonna fool 'em by keepin' it on the ground."

Baugh called 12 consecutive running plays, with fullback Andy Farkas finally scoring. Between touchdowns Baugh punted the Bears dizzy. During the season he had averaged a record 48.7 yards. Against the Bears he boomed a quick kick 85 yards. His right arm, his right leg and the right calls upset the Bears, 14–6.

In 1943 the Redskins and Bears again were matched for the championship. But early in the game Baugh was accidentally kicked in the head and suffered a temporary loss of memory.

"Use the 35 play more," Coach Arthur "Dutch" Bergman suggested on the sidelines.

Baugh gave him a puzzled look. "What 35 play, Coach?" Sam asked. "We don't have a 35 play." The 35 was a standard Redskin play.

"You better not go in, Sam," Bergman said. "Sit down until your head clears."

His head didn't clear until it was too late. The Bears won, 41–21. As it turned out, that was the last time Baugh would pass from the single wing formation. The next year the Redskins installed the T. Suddenly Baugh was behind the center instead of taking the ball a few yards back. It wasn't easy for him to adjust to the new system.

"You won't know it perfectly for two years," Sid Luckman, his Bear rival, warned him.

"Two years!" Baugh exclaimed. "How come it's going to take me two years. It's football."

"But everything's different. Your footwork. Your handoffs. It takes a lot of time, Sam."

Luckman knew what he was talking about. Baugh had his troubles with the T in 1944. But by 1945 he had mastered it and the Redskins regained the Eastern title. The Cleveland Rams, soon to move to Los Angeles, won the Western crown.

The championship game was in Cleveland in near-zero weather. Early in the first period Baugh tried his daring maneuver of passing from the end zone. But it backfired and the ball hit the goal post. The Rams were awarded an automatic two-point safety. It cost the Redskins the game, 15–14.

"I'm sorry about that pass that hit the goal post," Baugh told owner George Preston Marshall after the game. "Real sorry."

"Forget it, Sam," Marshall said. "Those things happen. But what's this I hear about the new league trying to sign you up."

The All-America Conference was being organized to begin competition in 1946 as an outlaw rival of the NFL. The previous day, in fact, many of the Cleveland Rams had received offers from the new Cleveland Browns of the AAC. Sam Baugh would be a prize catch for some AAC team.

"If a football player wants to jump the Redskins," Baugh replied, "he's the kind of football player the Redskins don't really want."

Baugh's loyalty was admirable—much more admirable than the ability of some of his teammates throughout the remaining years of his career. He would play on no more Eastern Division championship teams, although he did some great playing. He teamed with another skinny star, end Hugh "Bones" Taylor, to add to his passing records. But too often his team's pass-blocking would fall apart and he'd be thrown for loss of yardage. One night during those frustrating years he was asked to take a bow at a dinner for FBI men.

"Gentlemen," he said, "this is the most protection I've had all season."

Sammy Baugh had come a long way, both as a football player and as a personality. Once, while a rookie, he was so shy that he asked not to be called upon to speak at a football dinner. But the toastmaster double-crossed him. "And here," the toastmaster said, "is Sammy Baugh of the Redskins. Sammy, come up to the microphone and say hello."

"Hello," Sam said and sat down.

Baugh played through the 1952 season, but as early as 1948 he was threatening to retire. Arriving at training camp that season, a newsman asked him, "Is this going to be your last year?"

"Don't rightly know," Sam answered. "I'll see how I play in camp. For all I know, last year might have been my last year."

Actually, Sam Baugh would have his greatest day during that 1948 season when the Washington team and its fans honored him by celebrating a special Sam Baugh Day. In the game played on that occasion, the Chicago Cardinals were greatly favored over the Redskins, who had lost five games in a row. The Cardinals were the defending NFL champions. But Sam Baugh riddled them. He completed 25 of 33 passes for 355 yards and six touchdowns in a 44–21 upset.

Baugh's stature is secure. He finished his career with a total of 1,709 completions in 3,016 attempts for a .567 average. His passes gained 22,085 yards and produced 187 touchdowns.

Sam Baugh's finest tribute may have come from one of his blockers, Joe Tereshinki, in the Redskin dressing room on Sam Baugh Day. Baugh had gone on the field early to receive his gifts.

"This is Sam's Day," Tereshinki roared at his teammates. "So let's make it a big one. Keep those pass rushers off him. We owe him that much on his Day after all he's done for us. He's the greatest passer we'll ever see."

Sid Luckman
3

When the Chicago Bears won the 1963 National Football League championship, their quarterback was Bill Wade. But Wade was playing in the shadow of the man who has haunted every Bear quarterback for nearly two decades. The man is Sid Luckman. Bill Wade did all a quarterback can do in leading his team to the NFL title. But it wasn't enough to make the Bear fans forget Sid Luckman. One day during that season Wade was studying his playbook in the locker room when a newsman cornered him.

"What's it like," the newsman asked, "to find yourself being compared with Luckman all the time?"

"It's flattering," Wade said, "but it's not fair. The challenge to every Bear quarterback is the challenge of Sid Luckman. The fans here in Chicago look down on the field and wish they could see Luckman in his black jersey with the big 42 on it. But they never will see anybody like him again. I'm not another Sid Luckman. Nobody else is going to be, either."

Bill Wade's comment may have been Sid Luckman's finest tribute. Certainly no quarterback ever will be quite like Sid Luckman.

Billy Wade

Sid Luckman

Now a member of the National Pro Football Hall of Fame, Sid Luckman was the first quarterback to master the tricky techniques of the T formation. He mastered them so well that he became the symbol of the Bear domination of the NFL. During a seven-season span from 1940 through 1946, the Bears won four NFL championships and five Western Division titles. The first year of their reign, they massacred the Washington Redskins, 73–0, in the playoff game. This convinced football people everywhere that the T formation was the most explosive offense in the game's history. Until that game the single wing had been the basic offensive system. Now it is considered old-fashioned football. Almost every team uses the T formation popularized by the Chicago Bears while Sid Luckman was at quarterback.

Luckman was more than a wonderful football player. He always has been a wonderfully warm human being. Among other things, he knows how to win graciously.

As an assistant coach with the Chicago Bears, Luckman watched his offensive crush the Baltimore Colts, 57–0, in 1962. After the game he entered the Colt dressing room to talk to Johnny Unitas.

"Don't let this game get you down, John," Luckman said. "These things happen every so often. You're still a great quarterback."

"Thanks for coming in, Sid. I appreciate this."
After Luckman left, Unitas told a friend, "There
goes a real great guy."

Sid Luckman was the same way as a player.
Perhaps his best day occurred in 1943 against the
New York Giants in the old Polo Grounds. He was
a hero in New York, where he had been a college
star at Columbia. Earlier he had been a high-
school star at Erasmus Hall in his hometown,
Brooklyn. His many New York friends decided to
honor him with a "Day." Before the Giant game
he was presented with two $1,000 War Bonds.
Usually when a player is given a "Day" he can't
do anything right once the festivities are over. But
on this day, Sid Luckman couldn't do anything
wrong.

He threw seven touchdown passes, breaking
Sammy Baugh's record of six. Even the Giant fans
cheered.

When the game was over, Sid went into the
Giant dressing room to see their coach, Steve
Owen.

"I want to apologize," Luckman said. "I didn't
want to stay in there the whole way but the other
players wouldn't let me come out. I just want you
to know, Steve, that I'm sorry we rolled up the
score (49–7) on you."

42

"You don't have to apologize," Owen said. "If I'm going to be beaten, that's the way I expect a team to do it. Play their best all the way. I don't want anybody to feel sorry for me and punt on first down."

"Thanks," Luckman said. "It makes me feel better."

"It makes me feel better, too," Owen said, "to know that you were the one who threw seven touchdown passes against my Giants. If it had to happen, I'm glad you were the one who did it."

In addition to his ability, Sid Luckman possessed the knack of knowing how to inspire his teammates.

In 1944 the Bears, as NFL champions, played the College All-Stars in their opening preseason game. But this was during World War II and many of the Bear stars were in service. Luckman himself was in the Merchant Marine but he occasionally played on weekend leave. When the All-Stars jumped off to a 14–0 lead, Luckman began to tongue-lash his teammates. In almost every huddle he challenged them to play like the champions they were.

"Where did you men get these uniforms—steal them?" he snapped at one point. "These uniforms are not supposed to be disgraced."

Another time he warned, "I'll give some man—

any man—one more chance to throw a block. Otherwise I'm walking off this field."

On the play after the block-or-else challenge, the Bears sprung Ray "Scooter" McLean on a 27-yard run. They continued marching to a touchdown. The next time they got the ball, Luckman fired a 12-yard touchdown pass to Jim Benton to tie the score at 14–14. The All-Stars scored again, but Luckman engineered another touchdown. In the final minutes another Luckman drive ended with Pete Gudauskas winning the game, 24–21, with a field goal.

In the dressing room two of the old pros on the Bears, Clyde "Bulldog" Turner and George Musso, stared at Luckman.

"Sid," Turner said, "you are the greatest. You picked us up by our cleats and made us win this game. You're the greatest."

"Nobody else could have done it, Sid," Musso added. "I've seen you do some great things for us, but this was the greatest."

To Sid Luckman, it wasn't anything to be proud of. It was merely a display of loyalty to the team that had done so much for him. He proved this loyalty in 1946 when the Chicago Rockets of the All-America Conference tried to lure Luckman into leaving the Bears. The Rockets were offering him a five-year player–coach contract at $25,000 a year, several thousand dollars more than his Bear salary.

"I'm sorry, gentlemen," Sid told the Rocket owners, "but the Bears have done a lot for me which I can never hope to repay. I started my pro career with them and I want to finish it with them."

At a solid six feet and 200 pounds, black-haired Sid Luckman had the size and the skill to play pro football. But just as important was his instinct for calling the correct play. The Bear coach, George Halas, seldom bothered to send in a play.

George Halas taking notes during a practice scrimmage.

Halas realized that Sid knew the plays as well, if not better, than he did. In 1941, for example, the Bears were playing an NFL All-Star team in that year's version of the Pro Bowl. As the first quarter ended, the Bears were in a hole on their own three-yard line. Halas wanted to rest Luckman so he sent in second-string quarterback Bob Snyder.

"Bob," Luckman said on the sideline, "I have the six hole set up perfectly. Keep hitting it, and about every third play run inside."

Snyder followed instructions and the Bears marched 97 yards to a touchdown. Luckman not only knew which play to call, he called it quickly. This may seem unimportant, but it makes quite a difference in a game. Because Luckman was able to bark out the play almost immediately and hustle the Bears to the line of scrimmage, they were able to run about 10 more offensive plays per game than their opponent. Jimmy Conzelman, then the famous coach of the Chicago (now St. Louis) Cardinals, once said, "In those years, the Bears would average close to five yards a play. With Luckman calling the plays so quickly, it meant the Bears had about 10 extra plays and therefore about 50 extra yards even before the kickoff. That was enough to decide many close games."

Luckman, naturally, was in complete command in the huddle, as every good quarterback is.

Once, however, he delegated the authority of calling the plays. It happened in a game during the 1941 season. The Bears were on the way to a lopsided victory.

"All right," Sid challenged them in the huddle, "you linemen always think you're so smart. You call the plays."

The Bears had the ball on their opponent's 20-yard line. One by one, the linemen suggested a play. First the left end, then the left tackle, left guard, center, right guard . . . and on the fifth play, the Bears scored a touchdown.

"The right tackle and right end got gypped out of a call," Luckman said later, laughing. "But it proved I'm not so smart."

He was always willing to give credit to his teammates and always willing to take the blame, too. Once, in a game against the Giants, he couldn't do anything right. All his running plays were stopped. And when he passed, his receivers were open but he missed them. When the game ended, the Bears silently filed into their dressing room. Nobody said a word for a few moments. They were all thinking the same thing: *Sid Luckman has had a bad day*. But Sid Luckman knew it better than anyone else.

"Men," he said, loud enough for all of them to hear, "I sure stunk."

The Bears smiled. Now, instead of blaming Sid,

his teammates were admiring him for his honesty in taking the responsibility for the defeat.

There was something about Sidney Luckman that made people admire him all his life. Born on November 21, 1916, in Brooklyn, New York, he spent his early years in the crowded streets of the Williamsburg section. When he was five, his family moved. Because his father was making a good income with his trucking firm, he could afford a private home for the family, which also included Sid's two brothers and a sister. In the years that followed, Sid learned to play football in nearby Prospect Park. By the time he entered Erasmus Hall High School as a freshman, he was good enough to make the varsity. He was a substitute left halfback (the tailback position in the single wing formation). When he reported for practice as a sophomore, the coach, Paul Sullivan, took him aside.

"Sid," he said, "you're going to be my tailback. You'll do all the passing and the running. And I want you to call the signals."

Coach Sullivan made the proper choice. Erasmus won the Brooklyn championship that season. By the time Luckman was a senior, he was the most publicized high-school player in New York City. He was swamped with college football scholarships. But Sid wisely wasn't interested only in football. He wanted a college education, not merely a college letter. At Erasmus he had won the McGlue Trophy as the outstanding student in the senior class. Finally, he chose Columbia University in New York City, even though Columbia had not offered him a football scholarship. At the time of his decision, money was not a problem. His father could afford to pay his tuition.

Suddenly, his father's firm collapsed, a few weeks before Sid was to start at Columbia. Now he had to work his way through college. And work he did. He washed dishes in the college dining hall, scrubbed walls, delivered messages, even baby-sat. During the summer he was a lifeguard. During the fall, under Coach Lou Little, he developed into the best football player ever to come out of Columbia. He was a star passer and play caller as a tailback. But Columbia had weak teams. Even with Luckman, the Lions had losing seasons. As a result he did not receive much All-American adulation.

"No more football for me," Sid said after his final game as a senior in 1938. "I've had enough football. I don't want to play pro."

In Chicago, meanwhile, George Halas, the coach of the Bears, was studying the college crop of players. Halas was planning to install the T formation in 1939. He needed a passer, someone

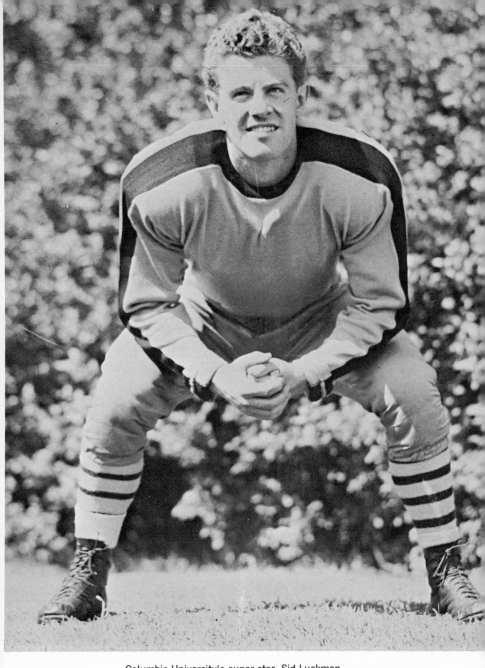

Columbia University's super-star, Sid Luckman.

who could be developed into a T quarterback. His obvious choice appeared to be Davey O'Brien of Texas Christian University. O'Brien was an All-America and the outstanding college passer that season. But Halas had secretly scouted Sid Luckman. He knew Luckman was three inches taller than O'Brien—an important factor in the T formation. He knew also that Luckman's family needed the money the Bears would offer him and that he would have an early chance at Luckman. Some months before, the Bears had traded end Edgar "Eggs" Menske to Pittsburgh for the Steelers' number one draft choice.

"You get an early pick," Halas told Art Rooney, the owner of the Steelers. "Draft that Luckman kid at Columbia for me."

This was how the Bears obtained the quarterback who would trigger the T revolution in football. Luckman, of course, changed his mind about playing pro football. Especially when Halas offered him a contract that, with salary and bonus, earned him almost $10,000 as a rookie. But when Sid reported to the Bear training camp, he had a problem: learning the new and complicated T formation plays. Halas assigned one of his assistant coaches, Luke Johnson, to tutor Luckman.

"The way you send those halfbacks into the line alone," Sid said one day, "they'll get killed."

"Don't worry, Sid," Johnson replied. "As fast as they get killed, we'll get you new ones."

As a rookie, Luckman was a second-string quarterback behind veteran Bernie Masterson. Halas wanted it that way. He didn't plan to rush Luckman into the job. The Bears had 350 plays. Luckman had to memorize them all. Often there would be several variations of a basic play and Luckman had to know each one. Halas knew that even a mathematical genius would need a season to commit all the plays to memory. So the old coach was willing to give Luckman plenty of time to absorb them. Sid was such a good student of football, however, that he not only knew his own responsibility on each play, he also knew the blocking role for each of his teammates. George Halas had selected the correct quarterback.

Other NFL teams realized that Sid Luckman was going to be a star. Although he played only occasionally as a rookie, the Brooklyn Dodgers offered $15,000 for him—unsuccessfully. Meanwhile, the quarterback whom Halas had ignored, Davey O'Brien of TCU, had developed into an All-NFL rookie for the Philadelphia Eagles.

"I'm glad for O'Brien," Halas said late that season, "he's a fine player. But I'm satisfied with Sid Luckman. You watch him go next season." Halas put Luckman at quarterback in 1940 and the Bears roared through the Western Division with an 8–3 record. One of their losses was to the Washington Redskins, 7–3. When the Redskins won the Eastern title, the victory set up a rematch in the championship game at Washington—perhaps the most famous game in NFL history.

In those days teams traveled by train. Ordinarily the Bears liked to play cards or read while their Pullman car roared across the countryside. But on this trip to Washington, the Bears were not wasting time.

"We all had our playbooks out studying our plays," Luckman recalls. "It was an incredible train ride. I don't think there were five words spoken the whole time. . . . We all wanted to win. That's all we thought about."

The Bears were determined. And when they arrived in Washington, anger was added to their determination. The Washington, D.C., newpapers quoted some of the Redskins as calling the Bears "cry babies" and "front runners." In the dressing room before the game Coach Halas didn't give the Bears a pep talk. He didn't even raise his voice. He simply held up the newspapers and pointed to red-crayon circles around the Redskin quotes.

"Gentlemen," Halas said. "We're not cry babies or front runners. Go out and play the football you can."

With a whoop, the Bears burst out of their dressing room. Now, on the sideline, Halas told Luckman, "On the first play, make it the pitchout to Bill Osmanski around left end." The Bears had the ball on their own 32. Luckman called the play. At the snap, he spun and pitched out to Osmanski who went around left end for 68 yards and a touchdown.

"The blocking was perfect," Luckman shouted to Halas as he came off the field. "It was just like we diagramed it on the blackboard."

The next time the Bears got the ball, Luckman sneaked across from the six-inch line after an 80-yard march. Soon after that, halfback Joe Maniaci broke loose for 42 yards and another touchdown. By halftime the score was 28–0. During the second half the Bears continued to roll. The final score, 73–0, left no doubt about it: the Bears were a super team and Sid Luckman was a super quarterback.

The Bears won the NFL championship again in 1941, 1943 and 1946—all with Luckman at quarterback.

The Bears keep hoping another Sid Luckman will come along. But even if one does equal him someday as a quarterback, it will take an extraordinary man to equal him as a human being. In recent years, Sid's basic income stems from an ex-

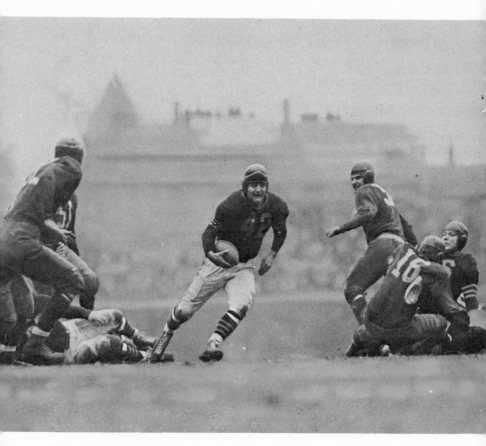

Sid Luckman charges through the Redskin line during the 1943 championship contest.

ecutive position with a Chicago cellophane company. He also tutors the Bear quarterbacks. When the Bears won the 1956 Western Division title, the players voted Luckman, as they do with all the assistant coaches, a share of their playoff money.

When Sid heard about it, he told the team:

"Men, I appreciate your thinking of me. But do me a favor. Take my money and spread it among yourselves."

The money was returned to the player pool. As Bill Wade says, "they never will see anybody like him again."

Y.A.Tittle
4

One day in 1962 the New York Giants were boarding their chartered jet airliner. The players, young and handsome, were being greeted by the pretty blonde, uniformed stewardess. "Welcome aboard," she was saying to each of the players. "We'll be taking off in ten minutes." Suddenly she was surprised to see a bald-headed man coming up the ramp.

"I'm sorry, sir," she said, stopping him. "This flight is only for the football players."

For a moment the man was surprised, too. Then he smiled and said, "But I am a football player."

He was, in fact, one of the greatest of football players. His name: Yelberton Abraham Tittle, Jr.

Fans everywhere had only to say Y. A. or Yat or The Bald Eagle and everybody would know whom they were talking about. He played seventeen seasons as a quarterback in professional football. His Giant coach, Al Sherman, once said, "Y. A. Tittle is the greatest passer of our time."

But the airlines stewardess could be excused for not realizing that Y. A. Tittle was a football player. Although he was a husky 195-pound six-footer, his baldness made him appear much older than the other players on the team. He even looked much older than the coaches.

On the football field, however, he created just the opposite impression with his bald head covered by a shiny plastic helmet. He had more pep than any of the rookies as he bounced around in his old-fashioned high-top shoes.

Y. A. Tittle spent most of his National Football League career with the San Francisco Forty-Niners. But he achieved his greatest success with the New York Giants after the Forty-Niners had given up on him. Three years in a row—1961, 1962 and 1963—he led the Giants to the Eastern Division championship. In 1963 he set an NFL season record with 36 touchdown passes. But his best day in football occurred in 1962 when he tied an NFL game record with seven touchdown passes. He fired pass after pass to such star receivers as

Y. A. Tittle

Del Shofner, Frank Gifford, Joe Walton and Joe Morrison. His blockers protected him, too. Usually a quarterback's uniform is smeared with dirt and grass stains, but Tittle's blue jersey and gray pants were virtually spotless. His blockers gave him the time to complete 27 of 39 passes for a total of 505 yards and all the Giant touchdowns in a 49–34 victory over the Washington Redskins.

Entering the fourth quarter, the Giants were winning, 42–20. Y. A. was waiting for Coach Al Sherman to rest him. On the sidelines, the phone to the press box rang. "Tell Al," a voice reported, "that Y. A. needs one more touchdown pass to tie the record." The message was relayed to Sherman.

Coach Allie Sherman discusses team strategy during a Giant workout. (Tittle is second from right.)

"Stay in there, Y. A.," the coach said. "You don't get a chance at a record like this very often."

The Giants moved to the Redskin five-yard line. In the huddle Tittle called for a running play.

"C'mon, Yat," said fullback Alex Webster. "Go for a pass."

"They'll be expecting a pass," Tittle said, "and besides, I don't want to show 'em up with a record."

"Look, Y. A.," said flankerback Frank Gifford. "If you don't call a pass, we're walking off the field."

Tittle surrendered. The Giants hopped out of the huddle. At the snap, he faked a handoff and danced back behind his pass blockers. Joe Walton, the tight end, cut toward the right corner of the end zone. Tittle led him perfectly. Another touchdown pass. Another record for Y. A. Tittle. When he retired after the 1964 season at the age of 38, he held NFL career records for most touchdown passes, 212; most passes completed, 2,118; and most yards by passing, 28,339. Quite a career for a Texan who learned to pass by throwing a football at an old tire hanging from a tree in his backyard.

Y. A. Tittle, the son of a rural postman, was born on October 24, 1926, in Marshall, Texas, a town of about 20,000 people near the Louisiana

border. While Y. A. was growing up, Sammy
Baugh was a star at Texas Christian University
and later with the Washington Redskins. Baugh,
a Texan, was the hero of every young football
player in the state.

One day when Y. A. was nine, he saw a news-
reel of Baugh throwing a football through a tire.
The next day Y. A. went to the town junkyard and
found the tire that would change his life. Hour
after hour he practiced passing through the tire—
from 10 yards, from 20 yards, on the run, standing
still. Usually his older brother, Jack, a star at
Marshall High School, was with him.

"You're a good passer, Y. A.," Jack told him
one day, "but you have to learn the rest of the
game, too."

"I know, Jack. But first I want to be a passer.
That's the thing I like best about playing football."

But passers need pass receivers. Y. A. convinced
his younger brother, Don, that he would develop
into a star pass receiver if he caught enough of
Y. A.'s passes. Soon Y. A. was learning to throw to
a human target instead of at an old tire. Later he
played sandlot football, and then he made the
team at Marshall High School. In those days the
T formation, with the quarterback directly behind
the center, was not popular. The single wing was
the most common offensive formation. In the single

wing, the best passer usually played tailback. And the best passer at Marshall High School was Yelberton Abraham Tittle, Jr. He led Marshall's rise into one of the strongest teams in the state.

When Y. A. was graduated in June, 1944, he received several college offers. He chose Louisiana State University in Baton Rouge. In 1945 the LSU coach, Bernie Moore, converted Tittle into a T formation quarterback. The next year Y. A. led the LSU Tigers to a 9–2 record and a scoreless tie with Arkansas in the Cotton Bowl. As a senior Tittle sparked LSU to a 7–3 record. He had many big games but at LSU the people still talk about the time Y. A. lost his pants in front of 40,000 people at Tiger Stadium.

Mississippi was leading LSU, 20–18, when Tittle, playing defensive cornerback, intercepted a pass. "I cut right in front of the Mississippi receiver just as he was reaching for the ball," Tittle wrote in his autobiography, *I Pass!* "We both had our hands on it for a split second and there was a struggle. I snatched the ball but he grabbed me around the middle as I started to run. He tore off my belt buckle."

In those days, football pants were loose and baggy, unlike the current skin-tight stretch type. Y. A. had a clear path to the goal line, about 70 yards away, but he could feel his pants slipping down. Holding the ball in his left hand, he grabbed the top of his pants with his right. He crossed midfield and kept moving—past the 40-, then the 30-yard line. At the 20 he tried to shift the ball to his right hand in order to straight-arm a tackler. With nothing holding them up, his pants dropped to his thighs. Then they sagged to his knees, tripping him. He sprawled on the ground 20 yards from the winning touchdown.

Everyone in Tiger Stadium was howling with laughter. Even Coach Bernie Moore. But not for long. Louisiana State University failed to score, and lost the game.

The episode of the droopy pants put Y. A. Tittle in headlines all over the country. But the pro teams had known about him long before. At that time the short-lived All-America Conference was the shaky rival of the National Football League. The Cleveland Browns, the team that dominated the All-America Conference, drafted Tittle. But he never played for them. Instead he was transferred to the Baltimore Colts, another member of the AAC. The move was an effort to bolster the Baltimore franchise. Tittle took over as the Colt quarterback, but after the 1949 season the AAC disbanded. The Browns, Colts and Forty-Niners were absorbed by the NFL. After the 1950 season, the Colt franchise folded (it was reorganized in 1953) and the Colt players were tossed into the NFL draft along with the 1950 college crop.

"Our first choice," announced Lou Spadia, the general manager of the Forty-Niners, "is Y. A. Tittle."

For two seasons Tittle played behind veteran quarterback Frankie Albert. But by 1953, Albert had retired. It didn't take long for Tittle to establish himself as the new boss. During a preseason game against the Giants, he got the Forty-Niners moving down the field. And he had halfback Hugh McElhenney, the NFL Rookie of the Year the previous season, running long pass patterns play after play. Finally McElhenney came puffing into the huddle.

"C'mon, Y. A.," he growled, "give us time to see how their secondary is lining up against us."

"If you don't like it," Tittle snapped back, "get off the field and send in somebody else."

McElhenney did just that. But their feud ended quickly and they became good friends. One of Tittle's most effective plays with the Forty-Niners was a screen pass to McElhenney. His most famous play, however, was the Alley Oop pass to lanky end R. C. Owens.

The Alley Oop was discovered by accident one day in a 1957 practice session. During a passing

Hugh McElhenny, one of Tittle's favorite pass receivers, runs a play.

drill Tittle found himself trapped. He flung the ball high into the air, not even aiming it at any of his receivers. Up and up it went, then floated down to where Owens was surrounded by three defensive backs. Owens, a star basketball rebounder at the College of Idaho, leaped into the air. With his arms outstretched high above his head, he caught the ball.

"Hey!" somebody yelled on the sidelines. "That's our Alley Oop play."

Realizing the value of such a maneuver, Tittle and Owens began to practice the Alley Oop. The next Sunday, against Los Angeles, the Forty-Niners were on the Ram 46-yard line with 50 seconds left to play in the first half.

"Alley Oop!" Tittle barked in the huddle. "R. C., get into the corner of the end zone."

Owens loped downfield. Tittle launched a high pass. The Rams were dumbfounded. Owens planted himself in the end zone, soared high into air and caught the ball for a touchdown. In the second half Tittle and Owens completed another Alley Oop and the Forty-Niners won, 23–20.

"Y. A.," Owens said after the game, "you just keep throwing 'em up there and I'll keep climbing up to get 'em."

Y. A. Tittle was selected as the NFL's Player of the Year that season. But the Forty-Niners lost a Western Division playoff to the Detroit Lions, 31–27, after holding a 24–7 halftime lead. As usual, the fans blamed the quarterback and Tittle was the quarterback. It was the beginning of the end for him as a member of the Forty-Niners. He struggled through 1958 and 1959. Then in 1960 Coach Red Hickey invented a new offensive formation: the Shotgun. In it the quarterback took the snap a few yards behind the center, instead of directly behind him as in the T. The Shotgun required a quarterback who could also run. The Forty-Niners had such a quarterback in young John Brodie. At the age of thirty-four, Y. A. Tittle had outlived his usefulness to the San Francisco team. The following spring he stopped at the Forty-Niners' office to talk about his future.

"Where do I stand?" he asked Hickey.

"I'll be honest," the coach replied. "We might make a trade for you."

"But suppose there's no deal?"

"Then," Hickey said, "you'll have to take your chances in camp. We're sticking with the Shotgun."

"I figured that," Y. A. said glumly.

As Y. A. Tittle drove to his Atherton, California, home that day, he knew that the Forty-Niners believed his career as a pro quarterback was finished. But *he* didn't think so. He reported to training camp and he played well. One day in August he was finishing his breakfast when a messenger from Coach Hickey stopped at his table and told him that the coach wanted to see him.

Tittle knew that it must be something important. He knocked on Hickey's door and walked in silently. He was waiting for the coach to speak first.

"Well, Y. A.," Hickey said, "we have traded you to the Giants for a young guard named Lou Cordileone. We need a good young guard around here."

Tittle had never heard of Lou Cordileone but the Giant guard had heard all about Y. A. When the head office informed Cordileone of the deal, he was very surprised. "Me for Tittle? Just me?" As it turned out, the trade was probably the most one-sided deal in pro football history. Cordileone didn't last long with the Forty-Niners. They traded him to the Los Angeles Rams, who later traded him to the Pittsburgh Steelers.

Before Tittle left Hickey's office, he asked a favor of the coach. "I'd like to talk to the other players before I leave," Y. A. said. "I've known a lot of them for a long time."

It was an unusual request. Players like to pack and leave quickly when they've been traded. But not Y. A. Tittle.

"Men," he said to the Forty-Niner squad on the practice field that morning, "I guess you know by now I've been traded to the Giants. These things happen in our business. I don't like it any more than you would. But I accept it. Don't feel sorry for me. I don't need sympathy. Football has been good to me. I owe everything I have to the Forty-Niners. And I don't want anybody to hold this against the owners or Red Hickey. They're doing what they think is best. If the situation were reversed, I might have made the same trade. Goodby and good luck. And thanks for everything."

Some of the players had tears in their eyes. So did Y. A. Tittle. He shook hands with them and walked off the field.

Returning home that day, he knew he had to make a decision. Should he retire or should he report to the Giants? His pretty brunette wife, Minette, helped make up his mind.

"If you retire, it's all right," she said, "but I know you would like to show everybody you're still a quarterback."

The next day he reported to the Giants. They had a veteran quarterback in Charley Conerly. But Conerly was forty years old. When Al Sherman welcomed Tittle, he told him:

"We didn't get you to sit on the bench. Charley can't go a whole season at his age. I'm sure you'll play plenty."

Tittle began to play plenty in the second game of the season. The Giants were winning, 10–7, in Pittsburgh when the opposition gave Conerly a bad shaking up. Tittle replaced him and completed four straight passes to score the clinching touchdown in a 17–14 victory. Gradually Tittle developed into the team's number one quarterback as Conerly's age became more and more of a handicap. Game by game, Y. A. began to pull together a championship team, something he had never been part of in San Francisco. His success became clearly evident in the final regular-season game against the Cleveland Browns.

"Four . . . three . . ." the New York fans chanted

as the final seconds ticked off on the scoreboard clock. "Two . . . one . . ."

The gun sounded. Y. A. Tittle was a member of the Eastern Division champion team. "This," he

Y. A. Tittle (14), still great after being dropped by the Forty-Niners.

would say on the day when he announced his retirement, "was my biggest thrill. There's only one reason why we play this game. To win. And I finally was on a winner."

Tittle had fulfilled another desire, too. He had proved to the Forty-Niners that he was still a top quarterback.

In 1962, when Conerly retired, Tittle was the full-time Giant quarterback. The Giants were *his* team. He led them to two more Eastern titles in 1962 and 1963. All three years, however, he was frustrated in his greatest ambition: to win the NFL Championship Game. Twice the Giants lost to the powerful Green Bay Packers. The other time, in 1963, an injury crippled Y. A.

In the 1963 game the Giants were playing the Bears in Chicago. During the first quarter Tittle moved his offensive unit downfield and threw a 14-yard touchdown pass to Frank Gifford. As he threw, one of the Bear pass rushers, outside line-backer Larry Morris, crashed into Tittle's left knee. In the second quarter, with the Giants leading, 10–7, Morris blitzed again. His helmet slammed into Tittle's left knee. Tittle went down in a heap, his knee ligaments badly torn. He hobbled to the sidelines and then to the dressing room. At halftime he told the Giants' doctor:

"Do whatever you have to do. Tape it up. Anything. I have to play the second half."

His leg wrapped like an Egyptian mummy, he walked stiffly onto the field. Al Sherman stood near the bench. "How does it feel?" the coach asked. "Do you think you can play or not?"

Tittle knew he couldn't maneuver properly on his bad leg. Passing is not merely throwing the ball. Footwork is important, too. The passer must be able to move quickly into his protective pocket seven yards behind the line of scrimmage. He must be able to plant his legs. Otherwise he is off balance. This ruins a passer's timing. But Y. A. Tittle knew the Giants were in a spot. Their only other quarterback was an untested rookie, Glynn Griffing.

"It could be worse, Al," he said to Sherman. "Let me go out and give it a try and see what happens."

Y. A. Tittle gave it a try. One of the most heroic tries in pro football history. If a player has torn knee ligaments he is usually required to rest for two or three weeks. But Tittle was playing in spite of them. He wasn't himself, however, and the Giants failed to score again. The Bears added another touchdown, winning 14–10. It was perhaps Y. A. Tittle's most courageous performance. But he never again would have the opportunity to win the NFL championship. In 1964 he suffered badly bruised ribs early in the season. In and out of the lineup, he ended up sharing the quarterback job with young Gary Wood. When the season was over, Tittle retired.

"I knew it was time to retire," Y. A. explained with a wink, "when Gary Wood asked me if he could have a date with my daughter."

Otto Graham
5

One day in January, 1965, Otto Graham was sitting behind his big glass-topped desk at the United States Coast Guard Academy in New London, Connecticut. As the director of athletics and head football coach, he was a busy man. When his secretary entered his office, he was poring over some paperwork.

"Commander," she said, "here's a telegram for you. It was just delivered."

Commander Graham slid a letter opener inside the yellow envelope and unfolded the yellow message sheet.

"Dear Otto," it read. "You have been selected for National Pro Football Hall of Fame. Congratulations."

Great Quarterbacks of the NFL

The telegram was signed by Dick McCann, the curator of the Hall of Fame at Canton, Ohio.

Graham laughed. "It makes me feel old," he said, "to be picked for the Hall of Fame."

It shouldn't have. At the time of his selection Otto Graham was 43—the youngest member of the Hall of Fame. He also was the member with the most recent qualifications. In 1955 he had finished his career with the Cleveland Browns—perhaps the most remarkable career of any player in pro football history. During his ten seasons, he was on a championship team *every* year. The Browns won their divisional title each season. Seven times they went on to win the league championship—three in the NFL (1950, 1954 and

Otto Graham plunges over the line for a touchdown, leading the Browns to a 38–14 victory over the Rams for the 1955 title.

1955) and all four (1946–49) in the old All-America Conference.

Handsome, black-haired Otto Graham, was six feet, one inch tall and weighed 195 pounds. He was also one of those amazing athletes with a winner's touch. In 1945, while waiting to join the Browns, he played basketball for the Rochester Royals of the National Basketball League. They won the championship—naturally.

He had been an All-American in both football and basketball at Northwestern University. But oddly enough, he had entered the Big Ten school on a basketball scholarship. He wasn't considered a football prospect until the coaches noticed him throwing touchdown passes in the intramural games. At Northwestern he was a single wing tailback. He didn't become a T quarterback until he joined the Browns. Tutored by Coach Paul Brown, he sparked the Browns' domination of pro football for a decade.

In fact, the Browns so dominated the old All-America Conference (AAC) that they ruined it. They were too good. They compiled a 47–4–3 record during regular-season competition and won all four playoff games.

In 1950 three AAC teams—the Browns, San Francisco Forty-Niners and Baltimore Colts—came into the NFL. Graham's reputation put him and his teammates on the spot. Throughout their championship reign in the AAC, there had been talk that they really were not good enough to play on an equal footing with the NFL teams.

The 1950 NFL schedule, however, had been drawn up in a way that put the Browns to an immediate test. In their opening game they were to play the Philadelphia Eagles, who had won the NFL championship in both 1948 and 1949.

When the Browns came jogging onto the field at Municipal Stadium in Philadelphia, they were booed by the Eagle fans, who made up a large part of the sprawling crowd of 71,237. The Eagles scored first, taking a 3–0 lead on a 15-yard field goal by Cliff Patton. And right away the crowd began heckling: "You're in the *big* league now. You're not playing semipros anymore."

Knowing they had to prove themselves, the Browns took the kickoff and began to march. They were on their own 41-yard line when Graham dropped back and fired a pass to flanker Dub Jones, who was slanting across the middle in Eagle territory. Jones was one of the fastest players in the NFL at the time. He caught the ball at full speed and outran the Eagle defensive backs to complete a 59-yard touchdown play. Lou Groza, the automatic "Toe" of the Browns, kicked the extra point. They were ahead, 7–3. Suddenly the

Philadelphia fans were very quiet.

They were quiet minutes later, too, when the Brown defense stopped the Eagles on the two-yard line.

"All right," Graham barked in the huddle when the Browns took over. "Let's get another touch-down, and we'll have 'em on the run."

Graham hit end Dante Lavelli on a 26-yard pass play, and the Browns quickly scored another touchdown.

Early in the second half, Graham completed four passes in a row to eat up 67 yards. On second down at the Eagle 13-yard line, he bounced back into the pocket, but appeared to have been hit solidly by big defensive end Norm Wiley. Graham bounced off Wiley, however. And when he saw end Mac Speedie free in the end zone, he pegged a perfect pass for another touchdown. The rout was on. The Browns won, 35–10, with Graham completing 21 of 38 passes for 346 yards and three touchdowns.

"Wow!" Earle "Greasy" Neale, the coach of the Eagles, said in the dressing room. "That's some team. And that Graham is some passer."

The Browns had convinced football fans every-where that they were real pros. Their AAC record had not been a fluke. That season they went on to win the Eastern Division title. But there was one more test for them: the NFL championship game with the Los Angeles Rams, winners in the Western Division. The Rams appeared to be a super offensive team. Using two quarterbacks, Norm Van Brocklin and Bob Waterfield, they had set 22 NFL records, including 466 points and 5,420 total-offense yards. But the Browns were slight favorites when they trotted onto the frozen field at Cleveland's Municipal Stadium.

The weather was cold and cloudy, the temperature a raw 25 degrees. It was windy, too, with gusts up to 30 miles an hour coming off nearby Lake Erie.

The Rams stunned the Browns on the first play from scrimmage. Glenn Davis, who had been an All-America halfback at Army, caught a pass at midfield from Waterfield and sprinted into the end zone for an 82-yard touchdown play. But on the sideline Paul Brown told Graham, "Don't worry about it. Let's play our game." The Browns quickly scored on a 31-yard pass play from Graham to Dub Jones. The Rams drove for another touchdown, but Graham came right back to fire a 35-yard touchdown pass to Lavelli. The Browns lined up for the extra point: Groza kicking, Tommy James holding. But a gust of wind blew the snapback away from James. He stretched to grab it, but there wasn't enough time to spot the ball for Groza. The Browns trailed, 14–13.

Early in the second half the Browns scored again when Graham and Lavelli teamed up on a 39-yard pass play. But the Rams rallied by scoring two quick touchdowns for a 28–20 lead. Graham wasn't finished, though. He fired a 14-yard touchdown pass to halfback Rex Bumgardner. Now the Browns trailed by just one point, 28–27.

With about three minutes to play, the Browns were moving again when Graham fumbled on the Ram 25. He came off the field, his head down, his eyes avoiding his teammates. But Coach Brown said, "That's all right, Otto. We'll get the ball back. We're still going to beat them. We've got time." Graham didn't believe his coach. All the Rams had to do was to get a first down and they would be able to kill the clock. But the Rams failed to get that first down. The Browns' defensive unit forced them to punt. Now the Browns had the ball on their own 32-yard line, and in the gloom the scoreboard clock showed *1:48* to play. This time, Otto Graham knew, there would be no second chance.

On the first play, a quarterback draw, Graham squirmed 14 yards. Then he hit Rex Bumgardner on the left sideline for another first down on the Ram 39.

"We don't have any more time outs," Otto

calmly explained in the huddle. "We've got to go for the sideline passes. As soon as you catch it make sure you step out of bounds to stop the clock."

He hit Dub Jones on the 22. Out of bounds. Then he hit Bumgardner on the 11-yard line. Out of bounds. The ball was brought in and placed on the left-side hash marks.

"This is a bad angle for a field goal," Graham said in the huddle. "Let's run the 36, Rex. Make sure you just get the ball in front of the goal posts."

"Why take the chance of a fumble on the hand-off?" Bumgardner suggested. "You can run a sneak, Otto, without as much risk." Graham agreed. "My hands were cold and wet from falling into a snowbank on the previous play," Bumgardner confessed later. "I was afraid I might fumble. I knew Otto wouldn't."

Otto didn't. He ran to his right and fell down in front of the goal posts. The clock showed 20 seconds to play when Lou Groza swung his square-toed right shoe. His 16-yard field goal won the championship game, 30–28.

The Cleveland fans screamed with joy. Their Browns were the National Football League champions. There was no doubt now that the Browns were the best football team, and that Otto Graham was the best quarterback. In the seasons that followed, the Browns would establish perhaps the most dynamic dynasty in sports history. With Otto Graham at quarterback, they would win six consecutive divisional championships. Including his AAC statistics, Graham would complete 1,464 of 2,614 passes for 23,614 yards and 174 touchdowns.

Significantly, after Otto Graham retired following the 1955 season, it took the Browns until 1964 to discover a quarterback, Frank Ryan, who was equally capable of masterminding an NFL championship team.

Lou Groza, the NFL's all-time place-kicking specialist.

Great Quarterbacks of the NFL

Many pro football observers consider Otto Everett Graham, Jr., the finest quarterback in NFL history. During his boyhood, however, there was no indication that he would develop into a wonderful football player.

Otto Graham was born on December 6, 1921, in Waukegan, Illinois, not far from Chicago. In that area basketball was the big game, and the Illinois high-school basketball tournament was considered the most important athletic event of the year. So even though Otto made third team All-State as a high-school football player, his real distinction came from being selected for the first team All-State basketball squad. He was the first Waukegan player ever selected.

In addition to his basketball ability, Otto was known as one of the four musical Graham brothers. His father was the music director at Waukegan High School and his mother was also a music teacher. As a result, all the Graham children learned to play an instrument at an early age.

His oldest brother, Eugene, took up the oboe and the English horn. Victor played the oboe, Richard the French horn. Otto, the youngest, was the most versatile. He played the piano, the cornet, the violin and the French horn. He was equally versatile in athletics. In high school he played baseball, in addition to basketball and football, and also took up tennis. He ran in track meets and was a good swimmer. In recent years, he has played handball and golf.

"I was born with good coordination, a gift from God," Otto has frequently said. "But I worked for everything else I ever got out of sports. There is no short cut to success. It takes practice. Too many kids like to think that because they have natural ability they're going to be stars. But it doesn't work that way unless they're willing to work hard to polish the skill God gave them."

Otto was willing to work. By the time he was ready to enter college, he had been offered several athletic scholarships—all of them for basketball. He narrowed the choice down to Northwestern, in nearby Evanston, and Dartmouth, in far-away Hanover, New Hampshire. Finally he chose Northwestern. In three years of varsity competi-

Otto Graham gains yardage for Northwestern in a game against the University of Michigan.

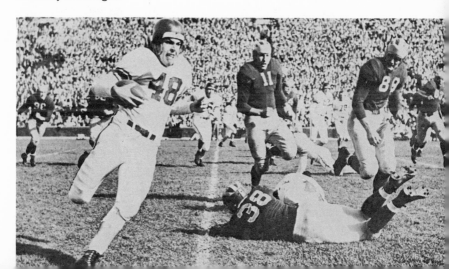

tion there, he won eight letters—three in basketball, three in football and two in baseball. When he first arrived he was considered such an exciting basketball prospect that he wasn't invited to try out for the freshman football team. But one fall day in 1939 he was playing in an intramural game when the varsity football coach, Lynn "Pappy" Waldorf, stopped to watch.

"Who's that kid throwing those passes?" Waldorf asked.

"Otto Graham, but he's a basketball player," somebody told the coach.

"He might be a football player, too," Waldorf said.

Waldorf invited Graham to come out for spring football practice. Otto impressed the coaches, but he tore a cartilege and developed knee trouble.

By the 1941 season, he was ready to play. At the time Northwestern had one of the most talked-about tailbacks in the nation, Bill DeCorrevont, but the unknown Graham split the job with him. Coach Waldorf knew he had something special in Otto Graham.

In 1942 Graham really started to attract attention. He outplayed Angelo Bertelli of Notre Dame, the season's All-America quarterback, in a man-to-man duel. But the Northwestern team didn't have enough other good players. A Chicago sportswriter wrote that it was "the best team ever to finish last in the Big Ten."

By 1943 Otto sparked Northwestern to second place in the Big Ten. Earlier that season he had played with the College All-Stars against the NFL champions, the Washington Redskins. He shook up the pros by intercepting one of Sammy Baugh's passes and running it back 95 yards for a touchdown. The All-Stars went on to upset the Redskins, 27–7. The publicity he earned in that game, plus his work at Northwestern, stamped Graham as an All-America. He was graduated in February, 1944, and entered the V-12 program for Navy pilots. The Navy sent him to Colgate University for a three-month indoctrination course. He was eligible for athletics there, so he played basketball and became an All-America for the second time. One day while he was at Colgate, he received a letter from Gus Dorais, then the head coach of the Detroit Lions.

"You have been drafted by Detroit," Dorais wrote. "This means that if you desire to play in the National Football League, it would have to be with the Detroit club."

The Lions didn't mention salary. At the time the NFL was the only professional league. If Otto Graham wanted to play pro football, he would have to play with the Lions—and on their terms.

But Graham wasn't thinking about pro football. He was concerned only with becoming a naval pilot. Sent to the Naval Pre-Flight School at Chapel Hill, North Carolina, he continued his training but he played football in 1944 with the pre-flight team. This was the season when he was first exposed to the T formation. One of the guards was Ray Bray, who had played with the Chicago Bears before entering military service. Bray helped install a few T formation plays with Graham at quarterback.

One day in 1945, after Graham had been transferred to the Glenview, Illinois, Naval Air Station, he received a message that Paul Brown had come to see him.

Otto Graham knew Paul Brown. While at Northwestern, he had played against Brown's Ohio State team. He knew, too, that Paul Brown had coached the powerful Great Lakes Naval team. But why, Graham was wondering as he went outside to greet the former Ohio State coach, was Brown there to see *him?*

Brown explained that a new League was being formed after the war. It would be called the All-America Conference and Brown's team would play in Cleveland. He wanted Graham as a T quarterback on the new Cleveland team.

"Don't worry about playing the T," Brown

advised him. "You've got the ability and we'll teach you the rest. We're hoping the war will be over soon so we'll be able to play in the 1946 season. We'll start paying you now—two hundred and fifty dollars a month."

"Now?" asked Graham.

"Right now," Brown said. "We've got the money and we want the best players. How about it?"

With Coach Paul Brown, Otto Graham holds the Robert French Memorial Trophy, which he received as the most valuable player in the Cleveland–Eagles game. Cleveland won, 35–10, behind Graham's spectacular passing.

"You've got a deal, Mister Brown."

When World War II ended in August, the Navy had no further need to train Otto Graham. He was soon discharged. But the AAC was not yet ready to go into operation. He played pro basketball that winter with the Rochester Royals, helping such stars as Bob Davies and Fuzzy Levane win the National Basketball League championship. "If Otto had stayed in basketball," Levane said later, "he would have been one of the great pro stars. He had everything. But he had his heart set on playing football."

The next summer Graham reported to the Browns' training camp. Besides him, there were such potential super-stars as fullback Marion Motley and place-kicker Lou Groza. It was the beginning of a reign that would destroy the All-America Conference and later boom the National Football League. And throughout the reign, Otto Graham was the man who played the most demanding position—quarterback.

"I knew I had to have a quarterback when we started the Browns," Paul Brown has often said, "and Otto Graham was the best."

Norm Van Brocklin
6

Stretching the big white "11" on his green Philadelphia Eagle jersey, Norm Van Brocklin had his
right arm cocked as one of his receivers, flankerback Tommy McDonald, cut toward defensive
back Bernie Parrish of the Cleveland Browns. It
was the opening game of the 1960 season and the
Eagles were moving toward a touchdown. Van
Brocklin threw, but Parrish broke in front of
McDonald and picked off the pass for an interception.

"Hey, number eleven," Parrish yelled every so
often for the rest of the game, "throw me another
pass."

Parrish could afford to needle Van Brocklin

that day. The Browns rolled up a 41–24 victory. But four weeks later, the Eagles and the Browns played again. This time Van Brocklin completed two important passes in Parrish's area. The Eagles won, 31–29. When the players left the field after the game, Van Brocklin tapped Parrish on the shoulder.

"That," Van Brocklin said, "will teach you to keep quiet until after the second time around."

Perhaps no other incident in his stormy 12-year National Football League career better illustrates the fiery skill of quarterback Norman Van Brocklin. He possessed one of the best passing arms in NFL history. He was an excellent punter, too, but he was regarded as a sort of freak. Chubby and slow, he could never have made the NFL except as a T quarterback.

"The only time I run," he used to say, "is from terror." His curly brown hair and dimpled chin gave no indication of the flaming competitive spirit that burned inside him or the many controversies that surrounded him. During that 1960 season "The Dutchman," as he is known, led the Eagles to a surprise NFL championship. But a few weeks later he retired as a player because of a bitter dispute with the Eagle management. He moved on to become the coach of the Minnesota Vikings.

Earlier he had been a star with the Los Angeles

Norm Van Brocklin

Rams and the hero of their 1951 championship team. But in 1957 he feuded with Ram Coach Sid Gillman. The outspoken Van Brocklin didn't like Gillman's strategy of sending in the play to be used. The Dutchman demanded that he be allowed to call the play in the huddle, instead of having it come from Gillman on the sideline. To solve the dispute, the Rams traded him to the Eagles.

"I wanted to coach the Rams," he said jokingly at the time, "but Gillman wouldn't let me."

Maybe Gillman should have. With the Vikings Van Brocklin quickly earned a reputation as one

Coach Norm Van Brocklin

of the best coaches in the NFL. "He has a mind like an encyclopedia," says Viking quarterback Fran Tarkenton. "He never misses a thing." As a player The Dutchman didn't miss anything, either, especially a mistake by a teammate. One of his Ram pass blockers, tackle Tom Dahms, once blew an assignment and Van Brocklin was smeared for a big loss. Coming off the field Van Brocklin picked up a paper cup of water and flung it in Dahms' face. Dahms weighed 255 and stood six-feet-two; Van Brocklin weighed only 205 pounds and was just an even six feet tall. As the water dripped down Dahms' face, his teammates waited for him to explode. But instead of turning on Van Brocklin, Dahms walked away. After that Dahms blocked harder for The Dutchman.

Van Brocklin had a sense of humor, too. He once used it to startle the Ram front office. One of the club's season-ticket circulars was mailed to him by mistake. In the box reserved for suggestions, Norm wrote: "Pay Van Brocklin a million dollars."

There's also another side to Norm Van Brocklin, a sentimental side that few people have seen. When he was with the Eagles, one of his best friends was the club physician, Dr. Tom Dowd. After the doctor died suddenly in 1959, Van Brocklin, who has three daughters of his own, gave a lot of time to the four Dowd children. One day Mrs. Dowd told him that she had to have the house painted but that all the estimates she had received were too high.

"Don't do anything until you hear from me," he said. "I'll ask around and see what we can do. There must be a cheaper painter."

There was. About a week later Norm Van Brocklin arrived at the Dowd home. He was carrying cans of paint and a supply of brushes. He put on overalls, climbed up on a ladder and did the job himself—free of charge.

He has a reputation also for being a soft touch for friends in trouble. Especially if they need a little money.

"I never keep track of these things," Van says. "They need it more than I do. Somehow it usually comes back."

Some years ago the Vikings made a 10-day trip to the West Coast to play in Los Angeles and San Francisco. Van left home with about four hundred dollars in his pocket. He returned with less than ten dollars.

"Everytime I turned around, I was passing it out," he says, "but it all came back. I was getting money in the mail for weeks."

Van Brocklin has a brilliant future as a coach, but he'll need several successful seasons to equal his reputation as a player. One of the most famous football coaches of all time, Clark Shaughnessy, puts Van Brocklin in a class with Sammy Baugh as a passer. The Dutchman had the knack of throwing a soft, easy-to-catch pass.

"It was like reaching for a bubble," one of his Ram receivers, Elroy "Crazy Legs" Hirsch, once said.

In addition Van Brocklin possessed amazing accuracy. In a practice session once, a Ram teammate challenged him. "Let's see how good you really are, Dutchman," he said. "Throw a pass

Crazy Legs Hirsch "reaching for a bubble."

and let it stop on the ground and see how close you can come to hitting the ball."

"Suppose I hit it?" Van said.

"Don't worry, you won't hit it," his teammate replied.

"But suppose I do?"

"All right, you get a Coke for every hit."

"You got a deal," Van said.

He threw a pass and it bounced to a stop about 35 yards down the field.

"You get ten shots," his teammate said.

Of the ten throws, Van Brocklin *hit* the ball six times.

"That'll be six Cokes," Van said.

"Dutchman," his teammate said, "I don't believe it."

"Easy," Van Brocklin said with a wink.

Norm Van Brocklin first began to attract attention as a passer at Acalanes High School in Walnut Creek, California, not far from San Francisco. Born on March 15, 1926, the eighth of nine children, he had spent his early years on a farm outside Parade, South Dakota. "When those awful winds of the early Thirties blew all the dirt off our farm," he recalls, "my father didn't wait to starve. He packed us up and moved everybody to California."

In high school Norm acquired the nickname of Stubby, and was a star in basketball and baseball, as well as in football. As a baseball pitcher, in fact, he was considered a major-league prospect. But when he was graduated from high school, World War II was going on. He joined the Navy at the age of seventeen.

When he received his discharge, Norm looked up one of his high-school counselors, an alumnus of the University of California.

"Is there any way you can help me get into Cal?" he asked. "I think I could play football or baseball there."

"Not a chance," the teacher advised him. "But I've got a connection at the University of Oregon. I'll try there."

Van Brocklin was accepted. He didn't have an athletic scholarship but he didn't need one. The GI Bill of Rights, as it was known, provided for the payment of a former serviceman's college tuition by the government. At the time freshmen were eligible to play on varsity teams. The Dutchman didn't waste any time. He made the football squad as a sub, and in the spring he went to the baseball tryouts. One day a college official called him aside as he trudged off the field after practice.

"Norm," the man said, "I want to let you in on something. As a baseball player here you can get work around the campus that will pay you about fifteen dollars a month. As a football player, you can get work for seventy-five dollars a month."

Van Brocklin took off his baseball uniform and never put it on again. He concentrated on football. But it didn't appear to be doing him any good. The Oregon coach, Tex Oliver, was using the old-fashioned Notre Dame Box offensive formation. Van Brocklin couldn't run fast enough to fit into that style of play. During the 1946 season, in fact, he played only three minutes and failed to qualify for a letter.

Then came the break that changed Norm Van Brocklin's life. Oregon fired Oliver and hired Jim Aiken as football coach.

Aiken had been successful with the T formation at the University of Nevada and he planned to install the T at Oregon. He needed a quarterback, however, and he had heard that Van Brocklin was a good passer. The first day he arrived on the Oregon campus he looked up The Dutchman.

"I understand you can throw the ball," Aiken said.

"Yes, sir," Norm said. "Some people seem to think I can."

"You might be my quarterback," Aiken said.

The coach shook hands with Van Brocklin. But as he did so, he picked up Norm's right hand and smelled the nicotine-stained fingers.

"No more smoking," Aiken snapped. "No more, you hear."

"Yes, sir," Van Brocklin said. "I understand, sir."

Years later, Van confessed, "He scared me half to death; I had to quit smoking." It must have helped. He took over Aiken's T formation and led the Pacific Coast Conference in passing for two straight seasons. In 1948 Oregon won nine of ten games and went to the Cotton Bowl. In 1949 Van Brocklin showed promise of being even better—or so the University of Oregon thought. So did most of the pro teams. But The Dutchman had earned enough credits in summer classes to graduate in three years instead of the usual four. The Rams, then scouting college players more extensively than the other NFL teams, had sent him a question-naire.

One of the questions was, "In what year does your class graduate?" Van Brocklin answered it by writing, "?"

His answer intrigued the Rams. One day Dan Reeves, then the Ram president, called Van Brocklin at Oregon.

"What does the question mark mean?" Reeves asked.

"It means," Norm said, "that I can play here in

1949 if I spread out my courses. Or I can graduate now and play pro."

"Would you play for the Rams if we drafted you?"

"If the price was right," Norm said, "I'd be glad to."

He needed the money. He had married Gloria Schiewe in 1947. She had been his biology teacher at Oregon, and had tutored him through the summer classes that enabled him to graduate early. His ambition carried over into the 1949 Ram training camp. At the time the Rams had one of the best quarterbacks in the NFL, Bob Waterfield. The Dutchman made the team but he had played very little until the final regular-season game, against Washington. Coach Clark Shaughnessy sent him in early in the first quarter.

Trotting onto the field, Norm was thinking of Shaughnessy's philosophy for a quarterback.

"Always remember," Shaughnessy used to say repeatedly throughout the season, "that being a quarterback is like driving ten mules. The mules are your players. You've got ten reins in your hand. You can pull them or push them or do anything you want with them. The quarterback runs the team."

But on one of his first plays, Van Brocklin fumbled a handoff. The Redskins quickly scored.

On the sideline Van Brocklin mumbled to a teammate, "I've had it. He won't put me in again."

Shaughnessy fooled him. "Norman," he yelled, waving his arm. "Let's get back in there now."

Encouraged by Shaughnessy's confidence in him, Van Brocklin settled down. He threw four touchdown passes that day and the Rams won, 53–27, to clinch the Western Division title. During the off season, however, Shaughnessy was fired. Joe Stydahar was coaching the Rams when Van reported to the 1950 training camp. Stydahar began to alternate The Dutchman with Waterfield. That season the Rams again were the Western Division winners but lost to the Cleveland Browns in the championship playoff. In 1951, however, the Rams defeated the Browns, for the NFL title, 24–17, when Van Brocklin and end Tom Fears teamed up on a 73-yard touchdown play in the final quarter.

In one game that season The Dutchman passed for 554 yards, an NFL record, against the now defunct New York Yankees. In another game against the Detroit Lions he threw four touchdown passes in one *quarter* as the Rams scored 42 points in 15 minutes, another record.

By 1953, Waterfield had retired and Van Brocklin was the full-time Ram quarterback. In 1955 he led the Rams to another Western Division title. But in the championship game against the Cleveland Browns he had six passes intercepted and the Rams lost, 38–14. "It was," Norm says, "the worst game I ever played. It still haunts me."

Sid Gillman was the Ram coach at the time. The next season Gillman began to alternate Van Brocklin with Bill Wade. Soon Wade was playing more than The Dutchman. And when Van did play, Gillman was sending in the plays. By the end of the 1957 season Van Brocklin couldn't stand it

"The Dutchman" (11) passes the ball to a teammate (21) during the Rams' 1955 championship game against the Browns.

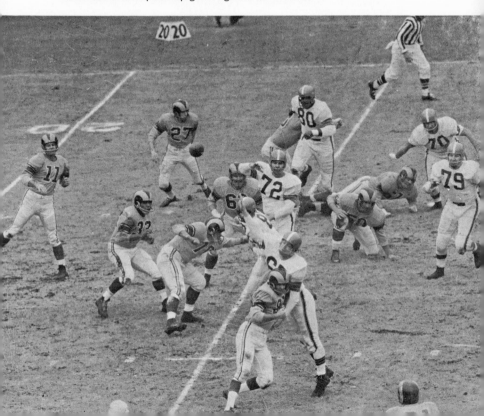

any more. He went to Pete Rozelle, then the Ram general manager.

"Pete," he said, "I want to be traded."

"I'll see what we can do," Rozelle replied, "but it will have to be to a team in the Eastern Division."

"Good. I'd prefer to go to Cleveland or Pittsburgh. Okay?"

"I'll let you know," Rozelle said.

Some weeks later the Rams traded Van Brocklin to the Philadelphia Eagles, a team The Dutchman had wanted no part of. The late Bert Bell, then the NFL Commissioner, had persuaded Rozelle to send him to Philadelphia in the hope of pepping up an ailing franchise. At first Van Brocklin refused to report. But the new Eagle coach, Buck Shaw, talked him into changing his mind. It didn't change Van, though. At training camp a newsman asked him:

"What do you think of your receivers?"

"We need better ones," Norm answered.

The 1958 season, his first with the Eagles, was the most miserable of his career. The Eagles put together a lamentable 2–9–1 record and finished last in the Eastern Division.

"The trouble with this club," Norm complained one day, "is that we got too many deadbeats on it."

Norm Van Brocklin

By 1959, the deadbeats were starting to disappear. The Eagles began to move up. They finished in a tie with Cleveland for second place, each with a 7–5 record. In 1960 Norm Van Brocklin led them to the NFL championship in a 17–13 playoff victory over the Green Bay Packers. It was the climax of a wonderful career and he did what every athlete would like to do: he retired while on top.

"I'm through as a player," he announced a few weeks later. "Too many players hang around too long. Not me."

But to everyone who ever had seen him play quarterback, Norm Van Brocklin didn't hang around long enough.

Van Brocklin handing off to Billy Barnes (33) during the Eagles' all-important game with Green Bay.

Frank Ryan
7

Inside Municipal Stadium the Cleveland fans were tearing down the orange goal posts in the cold gloom of late afternoon. The Browns had just stunned the Baltimore Colts, 27–0, to win the 1964 National Football League championship.

The Browns were celebrating, too. In the warmth of their dressing room, quarterback Frank Ryan was posing for pictures with fullback Jimmy Brown, flanker Gary Collins, defensive tackle Dick Modzelewski, and Coach Blanton Collier.

When Ryan finally made his way through the crowd to his locker, a newsman asked him, "How do you explain such a one-sided upset?"

"As you know from the principles of aerodynamics," Ryan said, his eyes twinkling, "it makes Bernoulli's Principle ——"

"It what?" another newsman asked, laughing.

Frank Ryan was laughing, too. He was using his scholarly background to needle the newsmen. For in addition to being a star quarterback, Ryan had also proved to be a mathematical genius. Already he had earned the degree of doctor of philosophy.

Sly jokes are typical of Frank Ryan. He laughs often. But on that day in 1964 when the Cleveland Browns ruled the NFL he finally had the last laugh. He had thrown three touchdown passes, and he was enjoying the adulation. For several seasons he had put up with criticism—first, with the Los Angeles Rams; then, with the Browns. But he had usually managed to laugh that off, too. For example, one day early in the 1964 season he took his children to the Cleveland zoo.

"It was wonderful," he said later with a wink. "The animals must be the only group in Cleveland that's not criticizing me."

When the Browns won the championship, the zoo animals were probably the only group in Cleveland that weren't *praising* Frank Ryan. He had emerged as a championship quarterback, a feat that even Y. A. Tittle failed to achieve throughout his long career. But just as a laugh is typical of Ryan, so is confidence. During the 1963

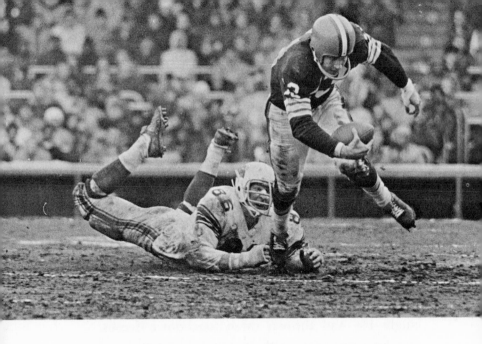

Frank Ryan emerged as a leading quarterback in the 1964 season. Above, he is being tackled by St. Louis Cardinal Don Grumm; below, he is firing his third touchdown pass in the 1964 play-off game with the Colts.

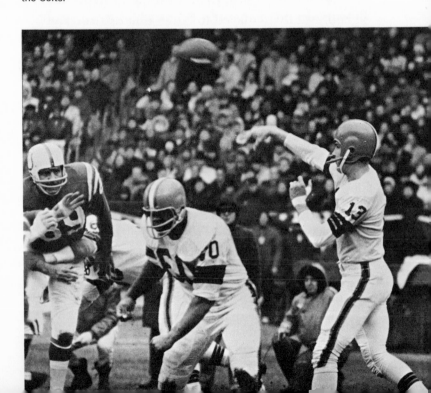

season he helped the Browns to a second-place finish in the Eastern Division. Awaiting the Play-off Bowl he sat in his Miami Beach hotel room one day and predicted:

"I'm going to be another Y. A. Tittle in two or three years. I think the experience will start to show up soon."

It did. And the Browns became champions. Their triumph was not a coincidence. Fullback Jim Brown had had a record-setting season in 1963, although the Browns failed to win the divisional title. But when Frank Ryan clicked, too, the Browns were finally able to go to the top.

Of course Frank Ryan is the first to recognize that Jim Brown is still the key player on the Browns. In one game the Browns had to run out the clock in the closing seconds of the first half. In that situation a quarterback would ordinarily have called a play requiring Jim Brown to carry the ball into the line. Ryan, who speaks in a whisper in the huddle, had a different idea.

"I'll run it toward the sideline," he said.

"Are you crazy?" Brown said to the slender six-foot, 195-pound Ryan. "Somebody will get a clear shot at you and tear you apart."

"No," Ryan replied. "I'll take the ball. I've got to protect *you* from injury, Jim."

"*Me?*" said Brown, whose 230 pounds appear to

have been molded from poured concrete. *"You have to protect* me?*"*

"No more talk, Jim," Ryan snapped. "That's the play."

Frank Ryan ran with the ball. And he survived. "He's as fearless a quarterback as there is in the league," Jim Brown has said. "He's almost frail, and he's a bleeder. But he's tough. Sometimes he's out there with a bloody nose, but I don't think he realizes it. He doesn't even wipe the blood away. Apparently he doesn't feel pain at all."

In addition to his bravery, Frank Ryan has a brain. He plays chess by mail—move by move—with as many as 10 opponents at once. It's as a mathematician, however, that Frank Ryan is somebody special among NFL players. His Ph.D. thesis in geometric function theory was entitled, "On the Radial Limits of Blaschke Products."

Hours, days and years of study went into Frank Ryan's Ph.D. degree in mathematics. The same study habits have resulted in his becoming a championship quarterback.

"He studies game movies at home throughout the season," says his wife, Joan. "He'll be at practice and meetings all day, then come home and look at the movies at night. It was the same way studying for his Ph.D. He was in class all day. Then he would come home and study until one

Frank Ryan

o'clock in the morning. I've never seen anyone with more stamina for studying. Whether it's math or football." To which Frank adds, "To me, the trick in studying is to shut everything else out except what you hope to absorb."

Ryan's sharp mind has enabled him to absorb a great deal. It also has enabled him to become pro football's most popular prankster.

Shortly after he joined the Browns, at their 1962 training camp in Hiram, Ohio, the club held its annual Press Day for the Cleveland photographers.

Frank Ryan as a Cleveland Brown.

"Where's Ryan?" one of the cameramen said. "He's new. My editor said to be sure to get plenty of pictures of Ryan."

The photographers surrounded Ryan and one of them said, "All right, Frank, pretend you're passing." Frank posed. In fact he couldn't have been more cooperative. He did everything the photographers asked.

That night, in an office darkroom, one of the photographers developed the pictures.

"These are the ones of the new quarterback, Frank Ryan," he told his editor.

"Hey, they're good," the editor said. "But, wait a minute! Ryan throws right handed. He's passing *left handed* in these pictures."

Sure enough, Frank Ryan had played a prank on the cameramen. They had to take the pictures again.

Another time he called up some of his teammates and, changing his voice, identified himself as one of the assistant coaches.

"No morning practice tomorrow," he told them, one by one. "Sleep as late as you want."

He went along with the gag for a few hours, but eventually he made sure to tell them it was a joke. Otherwise they would have been fined.

When Ryan was with the Rams, he already had earned a reputation as a brain. He had studied nuclear physics at Rice University and he was working on his master's degree in mathematics. During the 1959 season, on the night before he was due to start a game against the Detroit Lions, he walked in to see Joe Madro, one of the Ram assistant coaches.

"Coach," Ryan mumbled. "I've forgotten all our plays. My mind is a blank."

Madro leaped to his feet. "Sit down," he said. "Relax. Lie down on my bed. It'll all come back. You'll be all right."

"No, coach," Ryan repeated. "I'm all blank. I can't remember any of our plays."

Just then, Ram Coach Sid Gillman and his other aides, who had been listening outside Madro's door, collapsed laughing. They had put Ryan up to the gag.

Ryan's sense of humor can be so dry that sometimes he is taken seriously. This happened shortly after the New York Jets of the American Football League signed Alabama quarterback Joe Namath for a reported $400,000 salary-bonus package. Ryan, fresh from the Browns' 1964 championship victory, was in Los Angeles working out with the Eastern Division All-Stars for the Pro Bowl. Namath's contract was the big topic of conversation.

"If a rookie like Namath is worth $400,000,"

Ryan announced, "then *I'm* worth a million dollars."

He was trying to be funny, but newsmen reported it straight. As a result Ryan sounded conceited. He also sounded as if he were going to hold up the Browns' owner, Arthur Modell, for a huge salary. The next time he saw Modell he quickly explained what had happened.

"I was just kidding about the million," Frank told Modell, adding with a smile, "but I'll take half a million."

When Frank Ryan was a youngster, he didn't show promise of developing into a player who would ever be worth half a dollar among the pros. Born on July 12, 1936, in Fort Worth, Texas, he didn't play football until he was eleven. "My father went around procuring leases on land for an oil company," he explains, "and our family was always moving. We were in the Valley region of Texas for a few years and also in Mississippi before we came back to Fort Worth." But one day when Frank was in the fifth grade at E. M. Daggett elementary school, he joined a touch-tackle game at recess.

"I intercepted a pass and made a nice run," he recalls, "and I thought, 'This is really some game!'"

Frank Ryan

In the seventh grade Frank helped organize a 105-pound team named the Little Skunks. They went to the city finals, but lost to a team called Little Notre Dame. At the time, he was small for his age. Even when he was in tenth grade, he was only five feet, three inches tall and weighed just 110 pounds. He was on the *B* team at Paschal High School, but there were five other quarterbacks ahead of him. One day after the season ended, the coach held a squad meeting.

"Boys," he announced, "the following players will report to the *A* team at spring practice."

Frank Ryan waited hopefully, but the coach never called his name. His head down, he got up and was walking out of the room when one of the assistant coaches, Charley Turner, called him aside.

"None of the other coaches think you can make it, Frank," he said, "but I do. Don't say anything. Just come out for spring practice."

Frank Ryan's face lit up. At the time it meant just about everything to him to have Coach Turner do this. Little did he realize that Turner's encouragement would eventually propel him to the position of quarterback on an NFL championship team.

At Paschal High School, Frank Ryan progressed slowly. "I sat on the bench until my senior year," he says. "Then somehow I got a scholarship to Rice." Ryan sat on the bench most of the time at Rice, too. King Hill was the starting quarterback.

Ryan's college career perhaps is best summed up by what happened in a game against Texas A. & M. in 1957. The Aggies were the number one team in the nation at the time. With Ryan at quarterback, Rice moved about 70 yards to the goal line. But just then the third quarter ended. That was the signal for Hill's unit to come into the game. "All I had to do," Hill says now, "was sneak over for a touchdown. It was one of two touchdowns I scored that day and it set me up for All-America. I got a lot of publicity out of that game, but Frank made it possible." When it came time for the NFL draft, Hill was the prize plum at Rice. The Chicago (now St. Louis) Cardinals made Hill their first selection.

In the fourth round, however, the Rams selected Frank Ryan—much to the surprise of Frank Ryan. "I don't believe it," he told classmates when he heard the news. "I didn't think anybody would take me."

What Ryan didn't realize was that Bob Waterfield, the famous Ram quarterback, had scouted a Rice–Baylor game. Ryan had played only briefly, but he had completed four passes. Waterfield, seeing the ability the other scouts had missed, turned in a good report on him. The following spring, Sid Gillman, the Ram head coach, called Frank in Texas.

"I want you in Los Angeles on June twentieth," Gillman said. "All the rookie quarterbacks will be here."

Rookie quarterbacks are different from other rookies. Quarterbacks must know something about a team's offensive system even *before* training camp opens. This was the purpose of Ryan's early arrival. The Rams invited his wife to come, too, and reserved a room for the couple at the Sheraton Town House.

It sounded wonderful to the Ryans until they discovered the cost of hotel living in Los Angeles.

The Rams gave Frank nine dollars a day for expenses. "We thought it was a fortune at first," his wife said, "but we soon found out that breakfast for each of us cost over one dollar for only coffee and a roll. In Texas hamburgers were thirty-five cents then. The same thing was a dollar and a quarter in Los Angeles. There was only one solution. We had to sponge off somebody."

Bill Wade, then the regular Ram quarterback, noticed Ryan's financial problem and suggested that Frank and Joan join him and his wife for dinner. He explained to the young quarterback that there were a lot of restaurants in town where the owners were willing to pay for the meal when one of the Rams came in. If they were lucky, dinner would be free.

Ryan was lucky. Later he was even more lucky in training camp. One by one, the other rookie quarterbacks were cut. He made the team.

As it turned out, that was about the extent of his luck with the Rams. For four seasons, he was the second stringer. At the start he played behind Wade. Later he played behind Zeke Bratkowski, who had been obtained from the Chicago Bears in a deal for Wade. When the 1961 season ended, Ryan walked into general manager Elroy Hirsch's office. Some weeks earlier the Rams had drafted another quarterback, Roman Gabriel.

"I'm not coming back next season to sit on the bench," Ryan told Hirsch. "If you don't trade me, I'm quitting."

"I'll see what I can do, Frank," Hirsch replied. "But I can't guarantee anything. Deals are hard to make."

Shortly before training camp opened in July, Hirsch finally made the deal. Ryan and halfback Tommy Wilson went to the Browns in exchange for defensive tackle Larry Stephens and two draft choices. Paul Brown, then the Cleveland coach, made the deal but he did not benefit much from it. That season he alternated Ryan with Jim

Frank Ryan

Ninowski at quarterback. Then when the season ended, Brown was fired by owner Art Modell. The new coach was Blanton Collier, a calm, quiet head man. The change was to help Frank Ryan become a championship quarterback.

During the 1963 session at training camp, Collier took Ryan aside one day to explain his theory about passing.

"Concentrate on only one receiver," the coach advised.

Ryan objected. "But there are three and some-

Concentrating on one receiver, Frank Ryan (13) finds Jim Brown in the clear and passes to him.

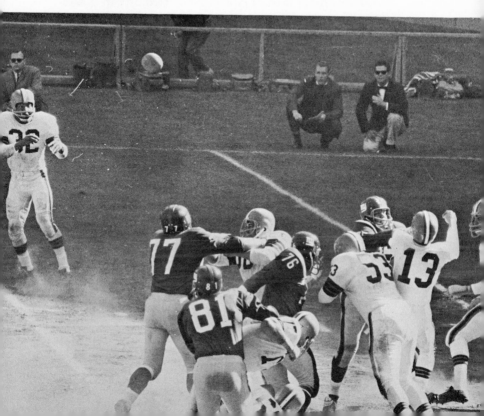

times four receivers on every pass play," he said. "I always thought I should look at two or three."

"No," Collier answered. "Only one."

"But why only one?" Ryan asked.

"Because you can *really* watch only one. Have you ever been in a railroad station or a bus station and watched somebody cross the waiting room through a crowd? If you follow him the whole way you have no trouble knowing where he is. But if you take your eye off him for a second, it takes a few moments to find him again, doesn't it?"

"Right," Ryan said.

"It's the same with passing. Watch one receiver and you'll hit him. Try to follow two or three and you'll miss them all."

"It makes sense," Ryan said.

Using Collier's theory, Ryan improved his passing. He threw twenty-five touchdown passes, tying a club record set by Hall of Fame quarterback Otto Graham. But in midseason he slumped. The Browns slumped with him and finished second to the New York Giants. In 1964, however, Frank Ryan did not slump and the Browns won the Eastern Division title.

It was not easy, though. It seldom is in the NFL. Entering their final game against the Giants in New York, the Browns could clinch the title with a victory or a tie. But a defeat would give the St.

Louis Cardinals an opportunity to finish first.

Late in the first half the Browns led, 17–7, but it was a shaky lead. Suddenly linebacker Vince Costello intercepted a pass and the Browns had the ball on the Giants' 48-yard line. Another touchdown now might break up the game. Ryan called a time out and trotted to the sidelines to talk to Coach Collier.

"Paul [Warfield] thinks he can get free on a Double Z Out," Ryan said. "I think it'll work."

"Fine," Collier replied. "Call it on the first play. Remember to give him time for his fakes."

On a Double Z Out pattern, Warfield was to fake inside, then cut outside and head upfield. There he would fake inside again and cut outside. But Warfield discovered he was running away from the Giant defensive back, so he broke his pattern. He hoped Ryan would spot it and adjust. Ryan did and lofted a high pass to Warfield. It was completed on the one-yard line. Moments later Ryan hit halfback Ernie Green in the end zone. The Browns led, 24–7, and they were on the way to a 52–20 rout, clinching the Eastern title. That day Ryan completed 12 of 13 passes for 5 touchdowns. His total of 25 touchdown passes led the NFL.

"This game," Giant coach Al Sherman said when it was over, "has to be the greatest Ryan ever played."

It was—until two weeks later when the Browns upset the Colts. Ryan's three touchdown passes made a hero out of flanker Gary Collins. They also put one of Frank's critics in his place.

His wife had received a letter postmarked Sandusky, Ohio. In it, a man had written that "the only thing wrong with the Browns is the quarterback." The letter was signed, but there was no return address. Joan Ryan attempted to find out where the man lived. But she was told that nobody by that name lived in Sandusky.

"It's all right," Frank Ryan told his wife the day the Browns won the championship. "You don't have to answer him now."

Bart Starr

8

Squinting in the glare of the flash bulbs, the Green Bay Packers were hollering and laughing. They had won their second consecutive National Football League championship with a 16–7 victory over the New York Giants in the 1962 playoff game. Now, as they celebrated in their locker room, newsmen and photographers surrounded Coach Vince Lombardi, fullback Jim Taylor, halfback Paul Hornung, linebacker Ray Nitschke and guard Jerry Kramer; everybody, it seemed, including the water boy. In the confusion a nationally syndicated sports columnist nudged a companion and pointed to a six-foot, 200-pound young man alone in front of his locker.

"Who's that?" the columnist asked.

"That's Bart Starr," he was told.

On any other championship team, the quarterback usually is the headline hero. But when the Packers were dominating the NFL with their two consecutive championship seasons, Bryan Bart Starr somehow was the forgotten man. So much so that a sports columnist, whose business it is to know the top players, didn't recognize him without his green-and-gold uniform. Many fans would not have recognized him, either. Starr's tight-lipped polite personality is responsible for this. There is nothing colorful about Bart Starr. He is, instead, a serious, retiring player. But as Norm Van Brocklin often says, "The toughest part about playing quarterback is winning." With Bart Starr at quarterback, the Packers win.

"And you don't win championships," Vince Lombardi once said, "without a real top quarterback."

Lombardi believes that a quarterback means "everything" to a team's offensive unit. Judging by Lombardi's own definition, Starr must mean "everything" to the Packers' offense. He has the arm. He can handle the ball. And he's smart. Brilliant, some people say. Many NFL coaches send in plays to their quarterbacks. "But out of the 65 or 70 plays that we run in a game," Lombardi wrote in his book, *Run To Daylight,* "I don't send in more than 10. He is great at picking that defense apart and adjusting. He has a great memory, dedication and desire. He is also a great student of the game."

To Bart Starr, being a quarterback is not something that begins in training camp in July and ends with the final game in December. It is also viewing game movies during the off-season. "It takes me about a week and a half," he has said, "to really analyze a game—play by play."

Starr has a gift for making a difficult situation appear easy. This was apparent during the 1962 championship game with the Giants. It was a bitter cold day; the temperature was only fifteen above zero at the kick-off and, degree by degree, it dropped to about five above zero in the final quarter. To make it worse an icy wind, sometimes blowing at a force of 50 miles an hour, swirled through Yankee Stadium. But Starr, although his fingers were numb with cold, did not fumble a snap or a handoff. He completed nine of twenty-one passes with no interceptions. He called plays which resulted in a seven-yard touchdown run by Jim Taylor and three field goals by Jerry Kramer. But typically, after he had held the ball on Kramer's game-clinching field goal, Starr showed almost no emotion as he trotted to the sideline

Bart Starr (15) fades back to pass during the 1962 Championship game against the Giants.

among his back-slapping teammates.

"I think," he said, holding his hands to the air holes on the side of his gold helmet, "my ears are frozen."

The previous year the Packers had played the Giants in the championship game at Green Bay. The morning of the game, his wife, Cherry, was so nervous she dropped a jug of fruit juice.

"I don't know what you're so nervous about," Bart said with a smile. "I'm the one who's got to play the game."

Bart Starr

Starr threw three touchdown passes that day but Paul Hornung, the Golden Boy, stole the headlines with a record nineteen points on a touchdown, three field goals and four extra points. After the game newsmen surrounded Hornung, not Starr. But in the coaches' room, one of Lombardi's aides shook his head.

"Hornung was spectacular," he said, "but the key man for us in this game was Bart Starr."

Starr is often accused of not being daring enough in his play-calling. But he is merely following Lombardi's orders. "I'd like to be a daring quarterback like Johnny Unitas," he says, "but the Packer system is conservative. We play ball-control football. We use a lot of running plays and short passes. We try to make as few mistakes as possible. It would be great to throw the long pass and listen to the crowd roar, but what good is a big roar from the crowd if it's for an interception?"

In recent seasons, however, Starr has begun to show more imagination. Midway in the 1964 schedule, he startled Lombardi with a bold call on a fourth-down situation.

The Packers were trailing the Cleveland Browns, 14–7, in the third quarter. They were on their own 44-yard line and they needed four *inches* for a first down. The Browns substituted some of their biggest linemen. They assumed that Starr would give the ball to fullback Jim Taylor on a power plunge. In the huddle Starr looked around at his teammates.

"We're going to fool 'em, Max," he said, meaning split end Max McGee, "I'm going to hit you over the middle. Stay alert."

McGee shuddered. The other Packers looked at each other. "Okay, let's go," Starr said, as they came out of the huddle.

At the snap, Starr faked a handoff to Taylor. The Browns' linemen rose up to stop the fullback. As they did, Starr took a few steps back into his passing pocket, straightened up and zipped the

Jim Taylor (31) takes a handoff from Starr (15).

ball to McGee, who caught it and burst through the startled Cleveland pass defenders. He appeared on his way to a touchdown, but he was hauled down on the one-yard line. Moments later the Packers scored the tying touchdown and went on to win, 28–21, over the eventual 1964 champions.

"That was Bart's call all the way," Lombardi said with a smile when the game was over. "I *never* would have called that one."

Bart Starr possesses another trait which pleases Vince Lombardi. He plays with what the coach calls the "small hurts." When Lombardi took over the Packers in 1959, he walked into the trainer's room on the second day of training camp to find half the squad lined up for whirlpool baths and diathermy treatment.

"What is this, a hospital!" Lombardi roared. "Don't you men know that you've got to play with the small hurts."

The trainer's room emptied. Ever since the Packers have played with the small hurts. During the 1961 season Bart Starr played with a big hurt —a painfully torn stomach muscle. He suffered it in mid-October, and it grew worse week by week. Eventually he had trouble standing straight enough to pass.

"Tell the coach about it," one of his teammates suggested. "That's a serious injury."

"The coach has enough troubles without worrying about me," Starr replied. "I can play with it."

Starr played so well that the Packers lost only one of six games while he was injured. That year he led them to their first NFL championship in Lombardi's regime. This success helped Starr develop the one thing he lacked at first: confidence, both on and off the field. When the Packers, for example, mailed out their 1962 contracts, Starr looked at what he was being offered and shook his head. He thought he should be paid more money.

Green Bay's great trio: Bart Starr, Jim Taylor and Paul Hornung.

The next morning he got into his car and drove from his Green Bay home to the Packer offices.

"Coach," he said to Lombardi, who also handles salary negotiations, "a couple years ago, I'd have signed just about anything you gave me. But now you've taught me to be more aggressive and self-assertive and you've given me more confidence. And this," he said, naming a higher salary figure, "is what I want."

Lombardi looked across from behind his big desk and chuckled.

"So that's it," the coach said. "Like Franken-stein, I've created a monster."

Starr smiled. He smiled wider when Lombardi gave him more money.

Another time Starr showed Lombardi that he was willing to speak up for his rights as a quarter-back. After the Packers won the 1962 champion-ship, Starr was among the players selected for the Western Division All-Star team in the annual Pro Bowl. There were eight Packers on the squad, but Lombardi didn't want to be accused of favoring his own players. In naming the starting lineups, he chose Johnny Unitas as his quarterback. When Starr heard about it, he cornered Lombardi.

"Coach," he said, "I don't like the idea of Unitas starting ahead of me."

"Why not?" Lombardi asked.

"Because I think I've earned the right to start. It's not just the idea of starting. That's not the point. The important thing is that I've been the quarterback of a championship team the past two years. I think I've earned the job on the All-Star team."

"But I can't have all the Green Bay players starting," Lombardi said. "It wouldn't look right."

"I don't agree," Starr said. "No matter how many Packers are out there, I think we've earned it." However, Unitas started the game.

Bart Starr has had to earn everything the hard way. Nothing came easy for him. Born on January 9, 1934, in Montgomery, Alabama, he grew up in an atmosphere of military discipline. His father, an Air Force master sergeant, taught him how to throw a football. "My dad never pushed me," Bart says, "but the big thing is that he helped me by going out in the backyard and playing with me. There are many kids who don't get that kind of encouragement from their fathers and it's a shame. I think it's one of the most important things in shaping a young athlete."

Starr first played quarterback for the YMCA's 100-pound team in Montgomery. He moved up to Baldwin Junior High School and then to Sidney Lanier High School.

One day during his freshman year at Lanier, he sat on the bench throughout the game. He was disgusted. He knew he was better than the other quarterbacks.

"What's the matter?" his father asked that night when he saw the sad expression on Bart's face.

"I'm not going to play football anymore," Bart said. "I'm not getting anywhere. I'm going to quit."

"Good," his father answered.

"Why is it good?" Bart said.

"The garden needs to be turned over and as long as you're not practicing anymore, you might as well do it."

Bart Starr changed his mind.

By the time he was a high-school senior, he was receiving All-America schoolboy honors. He went on to the University of Alabama. As a sophomore he led the Crimson Tide to the Cotton Bowl. But as a junior and senior he was bothered by a back injury. While Starr was a senior, in fact, the Alabama coach installed a youth movement—using sophomores and juniors, while Starr sat on the bench.

"It was ridiculous," Bart says now. "Any confidence I had built up throughout my life was almost shattered by sitting there and not playing. It took me a long time to get over it."

Between sitting on the bench and his back injury, Starr was not highly rated by the pro scouts. But Johnny Dee, then the basketball coach at Alabama, tipped off the Packers. "This Starr kid can pass," Dee wrote in a letter to a friend in the Packer organization. "And he's a bright kid, too, an *A* student. He's worth drafting."

Through sixteen rounds, no NFL team drafted Starr. But the Packers made him their number seventeen choice for the 1956 season.

In those years, Green Bay was known as the "Siberia" of pro football. No player wanted to join the Packers' team. Not only was it a bad team, but the small-town atmosphere of Green Bay was hard on the players. However, Bart Starr didn't care. He wanted to play pro football, so as far as he was concerned Green Bay was wonderful.

At that time the Packer quarterback was Tobin Rote. But Starr made the team as his substitute.

He also acquired a reputation as a member of Phi Beta Kappa, the national college honor society. Actually, Starr had *not* been a member at the University of Alabama. But when his playful roommate, offensive end Gary Knafelc, heard that Starr had been an *A* student, he started the story about Phi Beta Kappa.

"What are you doing that for, Gary?" Starr said to him one day. "You know it's not true."

"It'll help, you'll see. By the time I'm through, people will think you're a Rhodes Scholar."

In Starr's second season, the Packers traded Rote to the Detroit Lions. Rote later told newsmen, "Give Starr time and he'll make a winner out of the Packers." But the Packers then didn't have the time. They obtained Vito "Babe" Parilli from the Cleveland Browns. It was a strange combination. When Starr was a high-school star, his idol had been Parilli, then an All-America at the University of Kentucky. He had pasted pictures of Parilli on his bedroom mirror. Now, suddenly, they were teammates.

Parilli and Starr shared the quarterback job, but the Packers went nowhere. The next season, 1958, was even worse. The Packers finished last in the Western Division with a 1–10–1 record. Also, Starr was injured. Another quarterback, Joe Francis, had taken over as starter by the time the schedule ended.

In 1959 when Vince Lombardi became coach, one of the first things he did was to make a trade with the St. Louis Cardinals for quarterback Lamar McHan. Starr knew at once that he was in trouble. When training camp began, he was in even more trouble. During the first scrimmage, he faded back and fired a pass. But it was intercepted.

Vince Lombardi

"Starr!" Lombardi bellowed. "You could see that the ball was going to be intercepted when you threw it. One more like that and you're gone."

Starr skidded to third string, behind McHan and Francis. (Parilli had departed earlier.) But late in the season, Bart's luck changed. McHan was injured and Lombardi became less enthusiastic about Francis. The coach decided to give Starr an opportunity to play. It was a last chance. If Starr didn't produce, he was through. He knew it.

"I realized I had to show something so that the the coach would go along with me the next season," he says now. "Coach Lombardi has a favorite phrase—mentally tough. At that time I wasn't mentally tough. But I like to think that I developed a mental toughness at the end of that 1959 season."

With Starr at quarterback, the Packers finished with four consecutive victories. The next season Bart put McHan on the bench to stay, and led the Packers to the 1960 Western Division title. But the Packers lost to the Philadelphia Eagles, 17–13, in the championship playoff. "Starr," the whispers went, "isn't good enough." Vince Lombardi, however, didn't believe the whispers.

During the off-season Lombardi traded Lamar McHan to the Baltimore Colts. Obviously, Bart Starr was now *the* Packer quarterback.

Starr fulfilled Lombardi's faith in him by helping the Packers win the NFL championship in both 1961 and 1962. And early in the 1961 season, he convinced his teammates that he was there to stay. Up until that time he had been quiet, almost silent, on the field no matter how often he was

slammed to the ground by clawing pass rushers. But in a game with the Chicago Bears, linebacker Bill George crashed into Starr. Somehow George's elbow slammed into Bart's mouth. The impact jarred his front teeth into his lower lip. The blood was trickling out of Starr's mouth as George stood over him.

"Starr," the big Bear linebacker growled, "we're going to give this to you on every play."

"Go right ahead," Starr snarled. "The more you rush me, the more passes I'll complete."

Starr got to his feet and strode into the Packer huddle. His teammates had heard it all. They respected him for it. More important, Bill George and the Bears respected him for it, too. Typical of Bart Starr, he had earned this respect in a calm, dignified manner. Season by season, he would continue to earn more respect the same way.

With new-found confidence, Starr grins as he gains yardage for Green Bay.

Fran Tarkenton

9

Sweating in the summer sun, the Minnesota Viking players finished their laps around the goal posts, trotted to a stop and, in twos and threes, straggled off the field at their Bemidji, Minnesota, training camp. They were preparing for their inaugural 1961 season. Another punishing practice session was behind them. But one player, rookie Francis Tarkenton, stood in the middle of the field, his head bowed, the sweat dripping down his face, his breath coming in gasps.

"Tired, Francis?" asked Coach Norm Van Brocklin.

Francis Tarkenton was tired. But he knew what Van Brocklin meant. He knew the coach was waiting for their private workout, which had become part of the daily routine.

"Rookie receivers stay, too," the coach yelled.

Tarkenton stood erect and walked over to where several footballs had been gathered. "Okay," he said to the coach. "I'm ready."

"Remember," Van Brocklin said. "Seven yards, not five."

Tarkenton hunched, as if he were taking the snap from center. "Square out on two," he shouted, indicating the pattern he wanted the receiver to run and the snap signal. "Hut . . . hut . . ." He spun and dropped back seven yards, not five, pumped his arm and threw.

"You're floating it," Van Brocklin growled. "You've got to zip it. They'll steal that floater every time."

The workout dragged on as Tarkenton called the various patterns and practiced zipping his passes. Finally, after fifteen minutes, Van Brocklin said, "Okay, that's it." As they walked off the field together Van Brocklin said, "Francis, you're getting the idea."

"Thank you, sir," Tarkenton answered, "it's a pleasure to work with you."

Several weeks later the pleasure was all Van Brocklin's. The newly organized Vikings played their first regular-season game. Their opponents were the Chicago Bears. Everyone expected that the Vikings would be routed. But by then Francis Tarkenton really had the idea. In perhaps the most spectacular debut of any NFL rookie, he threw four touchdown passes, scored another touchdown himself and the Vikings routed the Bears, 37–13.

"It was fantastic," Commissioner Pete Rozelle said to Van Brocklin in the dressing room. "Imagine a victory like this in your first game. And Tarkenton! What a rookie!"

For Fran Tarkenton, it was the start of a storybook career. The son of a Methodist minister, he has a choir-boy look about him. So much so that Gino Marchetti, the NFL's most feared defensive end during his playing days with the Baltimore Colts, once described him as "that little boy." He's not really little. He's a solid six-feet and weighs 190 pounds, but his sandy hair and young face make people think of a little boy. Opponents, though, are no longer fooled by his angelic appearance. His ability to zigzag away from pass-rushing pachyderms has originated a new breed of quarterback: The Scrambler. Off the field, he is a highly principled young man who doesn't drink or smoke. But he doesn't wear his religion on the sleeve of his purple-and-white Viking jersey.

"I admire Francis," says one of his teammates.

"He doesn't sacrifice his principles, but he doesn't go around preaching. He's a real man."

Norm Van Brocklin admires Fran Tarkenton, too, but the coach who developed Fran from a green third-round draft choice into one of the NFL's most exciting players emphasizes another of Tarkenton's talents.

"Francis," Van Brocklin once said, "is faultless between the ears. He is a thinking man's quarterback."

He is also a players' quarterback. Several times he has been awarded a "game ball" during his Viking career. The game ball is a player's most prized possession because it is awarded by his teammates. They have fought on the field with him and therefore know who most deserves the honor. Usually Fran has received it for a spectacular performance, but once it was simply for his leadership. The Vikings had defeated the San Francisco Forty-Niners, 24–20, in their 1963 season opener and in a corner of the locker room, linebacker Steve Stonebreaker was saying:

"We gave it to Francis because he's a leader. He bounced back from two bad breaks in the second half—a fumble and an interception. He pulled the team together and scored two quick touchdowns. And this in turn inspired the defensive team. He's some leader."

Fran Tarkenton (10) in action during the 1963 season-opener against the Forty-Niners.

Coming from a linebacker on the defensive unit, this was high praise for a quarterback. But Fran Tarkenton is not always the type of player who can make friends with his teammates. As a quarterback, he must be the boss. Sometimes he must be a tough boss. He does this well, too. After a game with the Los Angeles Rams early in the 1964 season, Tarkenton was red-faced with rage. Hal Bedsole, in his rookie season, had dropped three easy passes during the game and the Vikings had lost, 22–13. In the locker room Bedsole was unlacing his cleats when Tarkenton marched up to him.

Fran Tarkenton

"Listen," Fran snapped at the big end. "If you ever drop three passes again in one game, you'll have to account to me personally."

Tarkenton spun and walked away. Bedsole stood there with his mouth open. Nobody had ever talked to him like that before. But several Vikings claim it helped make Bedsole one of the NFL's best pass receivers. In a way, it helped Tarkenton's development, too. There was a theory that he was too much of a gentleman to boss tough-guy pros. The Bedsole incident indicated that he could be tough when the situation demanded it.

The Vikings know Fran Tarkenton is tough on the field. So do their opponents. "Tarkenton," Johnny Unitas of the Baltimore Colts once said, "is a real money player. He's at his best when it's toughest."

For years Unitas has reigned as the best of today's NFL quarterbacks. But in the Pro Bowl following the 1964 season, Fran Tarkenton—not Unitas—was the quarterback who moved the Western Division All-Stars to a 34–14 victory. Tarkenton was selected as the game's outstanding offensive back. In addition to his skills, he thrills the spectators. This is primarily because he has a tendency, when forced out of the protective passing pocket, to scramble for yardage. Usually he scrambles until one of his pass receivers is open.

Occasionally he'll run to make yardage. When he first did this, he appeared to be risking injury. He once hustled 12 yards for a first down, but he was bounced out of bounds near the rival bench.

"Hey, Preacher," he heard a voice snarl. "Do that again and somebody is gonna break you in half."

This wouldn't be an easy task, however. By the time the defensive players catch up with him, they're usually too tired to hit him hard. Or they miss him. One day Gino Marchetti, weary from chasing Tarkenton that afternoon, slumped on a locker-room bench and explained why the young Viking quarterback was so difficult to catch.

"Every time he scrambles," the old Colt said, "it's hard on the defensive players because they have to run after him. You do that a few times and it can wear you out. And then you think you got him, but you don't. I thought I had him once . . ."

During the second half Tarkenton was scrambling as he looked for a receiver. Marchetti, six-feet-four and 245 pounds, was drawing a bead on him. Tarkenton was moving toward the sideline, his right arm cocked to throw. He couldn't see Marchetti thundering at him from behind. The Viking fans held their breath. Their little boy was about to be trampled.

". . . and I really cut loose," Marchetti con-

Gino Marchetti

tinued. "But when I reached out to tackle him, all I got was air. He was going the other way. He must have eyes in the back of his head."

Tarkenton developed his scrambling style out of necessity. For during his first few playing seasons, the Vikings were among the weaker pro teams. Naturally their pass blockers were weak, too. Also, their running attack was not feared. As a result Fran had to scramble to stay alive. But by 1964, with the emergence of halfback Tommy Mason and fullback Bill Brown as two of the best runners

147

in the NFL, the Vikings finished in a tie for second place in the Western Division. Tarkenton, meanwhile, had developed his scrambling style into an offensive weapon. In one game, he scrambled the Vikings into a victory.

The Vikings were losing, 23–21, to the Green Bay Packers with 54 seconds to play. They had the ball on their own 35-yard line, but it was fourth down, 22 yards to go for a first down.

All the Packers had to do was stop Tarkenton's desperation pass and they would take over, surely winning the game. At the snap Tarkenton spun and hustled into the pocket behind his pass blockers. Looking downfield for a receiver, he saw none clear. There was only one thing for him to do: scramble until he found a receiver. He circled to his right, faked a pass, ran up a few yards, swung to his right again. Behind him Packer defensive end Willie Davis reached out. His big hands were just inches from Tarkenton's back. But in that instant Tarkenton cocked his arm and threw. The ball was in the air when Davis hit him, smashing him onto the ground. As Tarkenton sprawled on the turf, he heard the Green Bay crowd moan, "Ohhhh. . . ."

The sound told it all. His pass had been caught. The Vikings had a first down on the Packer 21, a

"But in that instant Tarkenton cocked his arm and threw."

44-yard gain.

The Vikings killed the clock with two plays, then place-kicker Fred Cox trotted out and booted a field goal to win the game, 24–23. In the quiet Packer dressing room, Coach Vince Lombardi shook his head. "Tarkenton beat us," Lombardi said. "We did all we could. We chased him out of the pocket all afternoon, but he kept scrambling until he got the pass off. He was completing passes on plays half the quarterbacks in this league wouldn't try."

Tarkenton's talent for scrambling finally converted Viking coach Norm Van Brocklin. Although Van Brocklin sympathized with the necessity of Tarkenton's scrambling when his pass-blocking broke down, he didn't like it.

"Stay in the pocket, Francis," Van Brocklin used to tell him day after day when he was a rookie. "The only time a quarterback should run is from terror." But by the 1964 season, Van Brocklin had changed his tune. "We'd like Francis to throw more out of the pocket," Van Brocklin was saying, "but it's tough to keep a pocket when those guys bust your ears back and come in on you. And Francis has this ability to scramble around. It's a plus."

Francis Asbury Tarkenton, named after the

first Methodist minister in America, has been scrambling most of his life. And he has set an enviable record for himself.

He was born on February 3, 1940, in Richmond, Virginia, but he didn't play football until after his family moved to Washington, D. C. He was a member of the Merrick Boys Club team when he was ten. Oddly, he was an end, not a quarterback. "But I wanted to play quarterback," he recalls. "Living in Washington, I was a Redskin fan and my hero was Sammy Baugh." But his family moved again, this time to Athens, Georgia. There he began playing quarterback for the Athens YMCA team.

At Athens High School he was selected as the All-State quarterback. He had several scholarship offers, but he chose the University of Georgia, only a few blocks from his home.

At Georgia, Fran Tarkenton was a hometown hero. Perhaps his finest moment occurred in a game against Auburn. Georgia was losing, 13–7, in the closing minutes. There was time for only one more drive when the Bulldogs recovered an Auburn fumble on the Auburn 35-yard line. Tarkenton misfired on two passes. But the test of a quarterback is the third-down pass. He hit Don Soberdash with a pass at the Auburn 19. First down.

Another pass to Soberdash put the Georgia Bulldogs on the Auburn 10. But then he had a sideline pass broken up and a pitchout play lost three yards. Now it was fourth down, with only 32 seconds to play.

"I'm making up a new play," he said as he hunched into the huddle. "Billy," he said to left end Billy Herron, "you swing wide. I'll look for you. Otherwise the play is just a fake fullback dive. They'll be thinking we're going for the first down. Let's make it a touchdown."

Tarkenton clapped his hands; his teammates hopped out of the huddle. At the snap, he faked a handoff to the fullback. The Auburn defense converged on the middle. Herron swung wide and he was all alone in the end zone when he caught Tarkenton's soft pass to win the game.

Georgia posted a 9–1 record that season and won the Southeastern Conference championship. The Bulldogs went to the Orange Bowl and defeated Missouri, 14–0.

Despite Tarkenton's college reputation, the pros showed little interest in him. He was hoping that his boyhood favorite, the Redskins, would draft him and for a while, it appeared that they would. One day one of his friends told him:

"Look at this letter from George Preston Marshall (the Redskin owner). He's going to draft you number one."

Sure enough, Marshall had written to a friend at the University of Georgia. He had mentioned that Francis Tarkenton would be the number one draft choice of the Redskins. Other teams had contacted him, too, but only with a routine form letter mailed to all college senior gridiron stars. About this time the Vikings were being organized. They sent Tarkenton the form letter asking if he were interested in playing pro football.

"What is this?" he said to a classmate, noticing the strange Viking letterhead. "It must be a semi-pro team."

Unknown to Tarkenton, however, the Vikings had him high on their list of college players. The Redskins, meanwhile, shied away from him. They now were more interested in quarterback Norman Snead of Wake Forest. For some reason, none of the NFL teams selected Tarkenton until the third round. The Vikings had taken halfback Tommy Mason from Tulane on the first round and line-backer Rip Hawkins from North Carolina on the second. Tarkenton was their third-round choice.

The Boston Patriots of the American Football League drafted him, too, but Tarkenton spurned their offer.

"It's more of a challenge to me," he said at the time, "to see if I can make it in the best pro league."

Shortly after he signed with the Vikings, Van Brocklin sent him an official NFL football. "Get used to throwing it," the coach wrote in a letter. "It's different from a college ball. This one is fatter in the middle. Practice handling it, too. This ball is going to be your bread and butter."

At training camp Tarkenton at first appeared to be baffled by the complicated pro system.

"In college," Van Brocklin told him one day, "you probably had two pass patterns—the button-hook and the flat pass. Well, it's different up here. We got a million patterns and you've got to know them all. You've got to know them better than your pass receivers do. The hitch-out, the slant, the pivot, the flare, the take-off, the turn, the over, the come-up, the fan, the fog, the check-flare, the shallow-and-up, the wide, the wheel, the corner, the swing-and-up, the post and the cross. Got 'em?"

"Not yet, sir," Tarkenton said with a smile, "but I hope to have 'em in a few days."

"You've got to get 'em," Van Brocklin said, "because you must put all these patterns together to take advantage of the defense. You're directing traffic back there. And another thing, you've got to know defense before you can apply offense. Got it, Peach."

That was the coach's nickname for Tarkenton:

"Peach," short for Georgia Peach.

That season the Vikings had an experienced quarterback in George Shaw, and Van Brocklin was counting on using him as his regular. But in the first exhibition game, when the Vikings were trailing by three touchdowns, he sent in Tarkenton.

"Now listen, y'all," Fran snapped in the huddle, as he had at Georgia.

And he moved the Vikings, as he had moved the Georgia Bulldogs. He moved them to a touchdown, throwing a pass for the six points. As he trotted off the field, Van Brocklin slapped him on the shoulder.

"Nice going, Peach," the coach said.

In the next exhibition game Tarkenton played longer—long enough, in fact, to make the acquaintance of defensive tackle Billy Ray Smith of the Baltimore Colts. As Tarkenton threw a screen pass, Smith tackled him hard. Blood poured out of Tarkenton's nose. When the series of plays ended, his nose was still bleeding as he came off the field.

"Well, Francis," Van Brocklin said, seeing his rookie quarterback's blood-smeared face. "Welcome to the NFL."

During the remainder of the exhibition games, Tarkenton's education progressed slowly, but steadily. Meanwhile, Van Brocklin was working

Coach Norm Van Brocklin and his star pupil, Fran Tarkenton.

with him daily after practice.

"When we play those Bears in the opener," the coach kept saying, "they'll be coming at you like you were a piece of chocolate cake. You've got to learn this stuff."

Francis Tarkenton learned it well. His NFL opponents have learned something, too: the "little boy" is a big man.

Charley Johnson
10

During the 1962 National Football League season, Charley Johnson lived in a small apartment in St. Louis. Although playing for the Cardinals, he also was attending Washington University. One day, as he carried his brown and green textbooks under his arm, a curious neighbor asked:

"What do you do, Mister Johnson?"

"I'm a graduate student in chemical engineering, Ma'am," he replied in his Texas drawl.

"Good luck in your studies," the neighbor said.

Charley Johnson smiled and went on his way. He was studying to be a chemical engineer. But he also was studying to be the Cardinal quarterback. And in a late-season game that year, he threw five touchdown passes and scored another touchdown in a 52–20 victory over the Dallas Cowboys. The next day there was a close-up picture of him in the St. Louis *Globe-Democrat*. On his way to school that morning, his neighbor waved to him.

"I know who you are *now*, Mister Johnson," she said. "I saw your picture in the paper."

Opposing players are not quite so formal, but they know all about crew-cut blond Charles Lane Johnson. They know he is one of the best young quarterbacks in the NFL. They know he looms as a star quarterback for another decade. But in 1961, when Charley Johnson was due to report to the Cardinal training camp, he had to be talked into going. He didn't believe they really wanted him. Now the Cards wouldn't know what to do *without* him.

Complete dedication to football is believed necessary if a quarterback is to succeed in the NFL. But during his early years with the Cardinals, Charley Johnson developed into a star while leading a strange double life. Sometimes even a triple life.

He would get up at 6:15 A.M. and drive to a St. Louis radio station. There he would assemble sports news from the wire-service machines, write his script and at 8:00 A.M. his voice would come over the air saying, "Good morning, this is Charley

Charley Johnson

Johnson with news from the world of sports . . ."
Then he would drive to Washington University
for morning classes. In the afternoon he attended
the Cardinal practice sessions. In the evening he
returned to his apartment. After dinner, he would
spread out his chemistry books on the kitchen
table and study.

Radio announcer, student chemist, quarterback
—these are three difficult lives. But being a
quarterback is perhaps the most difficult of the
three.

There are thousands of radio announcers
throughout the United States—thousands of
chemists, too. But there are only fourteen regular
quarterbacks in the National Football League.
Not only is Charley Johnson one of those fourteen,
he also is regarded now as one of the best of the
current group.

His reputation as a chemical engineer does not
always make it easy for him, however. There is
nobody a football player enjoys needling more
than a scholar—especially if the "brain" is one of
his own teammates.

Once the Cardinals set up a news conference to
announce that Johnson and one of his favorite
pass receivers, Sonny Randle, had signed their
contracts for the coming season. The photographers had their cameras ready as Johnson and

Randle sat at a big desk with their contracts in front of them.

"Pretend you're signing it," a photographer said.

Johnson reached out to take a pen from its desk stand. The pen was stuck in its holder.

"Here," Randle said, "let me try it."

Randle wiggled the pen and it slid out easily. Turning to Johnson, Sonny shook his head.

"You're an engineer," Randle said with a grin, "but you need me to put the pen in your hand."

Johnson's chemical studies created a problem for Cardinal publicity man Joe Pollack. In order to answer questions from newsmen, he had to know the exact nature of Charley's work. One day in the club offices, Pollack stopped Johnson.

"Tell me," Pollack said, "exactly what you're studying."

"I'm concentrating on polymer plastics," Charley said.

"What?"

"They involve rheology," Charley explained.

"Translate it into English."

"It involves the characteristics of flow," Charley said with a smile. "Different plastics have different qualities of flow. I figure out the whys and wherefores."

"What's the title of your master's thesis."

Charley Johnson

"The expansion of laminar jets of organic liquids issuing from capillary tubes," Charley replied.

Pollack threw up his hands. "I'm sorry I asked," he said.

Charley Johnson poses for photographers after receiving his Master of Science degree in chemical engineering.

On the football field there is nothing complicated about the way Charley Johnson plays quarterback. He plays to win. The surprising part, though, is that he was the Cardinal regular in his second NFL season. Some quarterbacks need five or six seasons before they establish themselves. As a rookie in 1961 Johnson was seldom used. He was a third stringer behind Sam Etcheverry and Ralph Guglielmi. But by 1962, Guglielmi had been traded and Etcheverry was going sour. During the fifth game the Cardinals were losing to the New York Giants, 31–7, in the fourth quarter.

"Charley," Coach Wally Lemm said on the sideline, "go in there and do something."

Johnson didn't save the game, of course, but he did complete seven passes. The next week Lemm started him against the Washington Redskins. The Redskins jumped into a 14–3 lead. Johnson didn't panic but instead of using the game plan (the plays which had been developed to succeed against the Washington team), he was told by Lemm to switch to plays which might result in a quick score. The plays failed. Coming off the field at halftime, Johnson walked with Lemm.

"Coach," he said, "I think we might be better off to go back to the game plan in the second half."

Lemm agreed and Johnson rallied the Cardinals into a 17–14 lead before a late Redskin field goal tied the score. In the dressing room after the game Sam Etcheverry, the quarterback who had just lost his job to Charley Johnson, stood up on a red-and-white equipment trunk.

"The game ball," Etcheverry announced, "goes to Charley Johnson." His teammates yelled and applauded.

Ever since that day, Charley Johnson has been the Cardinal quarterback. With him, the Cardinals suddenly began to win. In 1963 they finished third in the Eastern Division. In 1964 they moved up to second place. But Charley Johnson, scholar that he is, realizes that he still has much to learn about playing his position. This was obvious one day during the 1963 season when the Giants, with Y. A. Tittle at quarterback, wrecked the Cardinals, 38–21. After the game Tittle was getting out of his uniform when he looked up to see Charley Johnson coming toward his locker.

"Tell me something, Y. A.," Charley asked. "What do you do when you seem to have lost control of your passes?"

Tittle was startled. He didn't know what to say. Finally he shrugged his shoulders and told Johnson, "Don't worry. You're gripping the ball all right. The main thing is to keep throwing. Don't get down on yourself. That's about all I can tell you. I hope it helps."

"Thanks, Y. A.," Charley said. "Maybe it'll help me." He shook hands with Tittle and left the Giant locker room.

Three weeks later, he used Tittle's advice. He threw two touchdown passes and the Cards upset the Giants, 24–17.

Charley Johnson possesses another trait that makes him a big man among the Cardinals. He's willing to say he's had a bad day. Late in the 1963 season the Cardinals had a chance to win the Eastern title. They were playing against the Browns in St. Louis. But the Cardinals lost, 24–10.

Finding no receivers, Johnson (12) elects to run, but Bill Glass (80) brings him down for a 7-yard loss in the Cards' disastrous late-season 1963 game against the Browns.

Charley Johnson

The team played badly, but Johnson was terrible. His passing yardage that day was 19. In the locker room he was surrounded by newsmen asking the same question:

"What was wrong?"

"We took too long to take advantage of the short pass," Charley explained. "They were giving us the short pass to the outside. But we didn't take advantage of it. I mean *I* didn't take advantage of it. *I*," he added sarcastically, "take all the *credit* for losing this game."

Until Charley Johnson developed into a star with the Cardinals, he seldom got the credit or the blame for anything in football. Most of the time he was ignored.

Born on November 22, 1938, he grew up in Big Spring, Texas, where the wind howls across the plain. Football is important in that part of Texas, almost as important as oil and cotton. His father handed him a football before he could walk. When Charley was three he threw it so well that his father, the city tax assessor, was asked to let him put on an exhibition between halves of a high-school game. But little Charley was too shy. By the time he reached high school, he was good, but not sensational. He didn't take over as the first-string quarterback until his senior season.

"There were eight schools in our district," Charley recalls, "and seven quarterbacks got some kind of All-Star recognition. I was the only one who didn't."

As a result Charley was unable to sell himself to any of the major colleges—or even to any of the minor colleges. He settled for a scholarship at a small junior college named Schreiner Institute. "I was so impressive," he said, "that after my first year, they dropped football at Schreiner." But Charley stayed to play basketball. Oddly enough, he received his first big break in a basketball tournament. In the stands was C. R. Bickerstaff, a scout from New Mexico State University. Sitting next to Bickerstaff was Charley's uncle, Jack Johnson, a friend of the scout.

"Believe me, C. R.," Charley's uncle kept saying during the game, "Charley can help your basketball team. And he can play football, too."

Bickerstaff's report resulted in Charley's receiving an athletic scholarship. The next fall, when he reported for football practice, New Mexico State had a new coach: Warren Woodson. In high school, Johnson had been a roll-out quarterback. But he really wasn't fast enough to make much yardage as a runner, which a roll-out quarterback must do. Woodson, however, installed a pro-type of offense, in which the quarterback dropped back to pass from the pocket. This, as it turned out, was ideal for Charley Johnson.

He was selected to the All-Border Conference team for three straight seasons. As a senior his 1,634 yards (1,511 passing) put him third in the nation in total offense. He was on two Sun Bowl winning teams.

Even so, he usually was overshadowed by his teammates. The pro scouts were concentrating on three other New Mexico State players—flanker Pervis Atkins, halfback Bob Gaiters and fullback Bob Jackson. The Los Angeles Rams drafted Atkins; the New York Giants selected Gaiters, and the San Diego Chargers of the American Football League chose Jackson.

The Cardinals had also been interested in Gaiters. One night during the 1959 season, two of the Card assistant coaches, Walt Prochaska and Chuck Drulis, were watching some New Mexico State football films. It was a few weeks before the college draft, and they were inspecting Gaiters. On one play Johnson bounced back into the pocket and threw a sideline pass to Atkins. The coaches looked at each other.

"Let's run that again," Prochaska said. "That quarterback might be the best of the bunch."

That year the Cardinals made Charley Johnson their number ten draft choice on a list of future

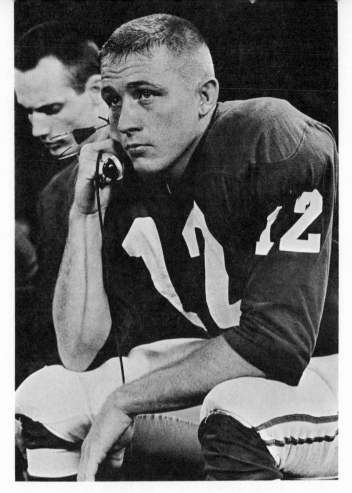
Johnson watches the action while listening to instructions from the St. Louis coaches in the press box.

prospects. They were willing to wait a year for him. Johnson, meanwhile, wasn't impressed at being selected. The next year the San Diego Chargers picked him as their number eight choice. One night Sid Gillman, then the coach of the Chargers, called Johnson to talk about a contract.

"I'm sorry, sir," Johnson said, "but the Cardinals are offering me three thousand dollars more than that."

He naturally accepted the Cardinal offer. But he still wasn't convinced the Cardinals *really* wanted him. One day, sitting on the edge of the bed in his dormitory room at New Mexico State, he was discussing the problem with Pervis Atkins and Bob Gaiters.

"I don't think I'll bother reporting," Johnson said.

"Don't you dare talk like that," Atkins said. "You can make it up there, Charley."

"No, I think I'd be better off going to graduate school."

"Go to school, too," Gaiters said.

"They just made me a token draft choice," Johnson said. "They've got five quarterbacks. They don't need me."

"Look," Atkins said, "if we have to, we'll drive you to that Cardinal training camp. Charley, you're going."

Johnson shrugged. "All right," he said. "I'll give it a shot. But don't be surprised when they cut me."

When he checked in at the Cardinal camp at Lake Forest, Illinois, there was a sign on the bulletin board: "Physical Exams Tomorrow." The next day, as Charley took his physical, two of the coaches were watching the players go through the tests.

"Who's that kid?" one of the coaches said.

"That's the quarterback from New Mexico State, Charley Johnson," the other coach said.

"He doesn't look big enough."

"The card says he's six feet and weighs 190."

"He doesn't look it."

"We'll find out how *big* he is in the first scrimmage," one of the coaches said with a wink.

As the fifth-string quarterback, Charley Johnson played only briefly in the opening scrimmage. But it was sufficient to convince the coaches and his teammates that he was tough enough. During one play veteran linebacker Bill Koman shot in and smashed Johnson to the ground with a hard tackle. Johnson went down, his body crunching into the turf. But there wasn't a whimper out of him. And just as important, the pass he had thrown gained 22 yards.

"This kid is all right," Koman told his teammates in the defensive huddle. "He might make it."

Charley Johnson did make it. But at the time he was merely another rookie who survived the cuts. The Cardinals were counting on Sam Etcheverry and Ralph Guglielmi. But before the 1961 season, Guglielmi was traded to the Giants, and Johnson moved up behind Etcheverry.

"I liked Charley's moves," said Wally Lemm, who took over as the Cardinal coach that year. "But there's no way of knowing how a kid will react until you play him."

When Etcheverry went sour, Charley Johnson got his chance. And he made the most of it. By 1964 he had gained such stature that Lemm was willing to be overruled in a crucial situation. In a game with the Redskins the score was tied 24–24. The Cardinals had the ball on the Redskin 12-yard line with 30 seconds to play. Calling a time out, Johnson noticed field-goal kicker Jim Bakken coming into the game. But Charley waved Bakken back to the bench and ran over to the sideline to talk to Lemm.

"Let's go for a touchdown," Charley said. "We have time."

"No," Lemm answered. He was afraid that if the Cards didn't kick a field goal on third down, the Redskins might pull something to run out the clock.

"But I know the short pass to Conrad will work." Johnson protested.

"How do you know?"

"They've been playing him deep. And if he's not open, I'll get rid of the ball in time to stop the clock."

Johnson (12) gets off a pass in the January 3, 1965, play off game between the Packers and the Cardinals at Miami, Florida. The Cards won, 24–17.

"All right," Lemm said, "go ahead."

Bobby Joe Conrad, the flankerback, broke clear on a short pattern and Johnson hit him with the

pass for the touchdown. The Cardinals won, 31–24. On the way off the field Lemm told Charley, "Good call."

The fans cheered Charley Johnson that day, as they have continued to cheer him almost every Sunday during the season.

About the Author

DAVE ANDERSON, a sports writer for the New York *Journal-American*, has been covering professional football for many years, and has written articles for the *Saturday Evening Post, True, Sports Illustrated* and *Sport* magazine. He is also the author of the *Pro Football Handbook* and *The Major League Baseball Handbook* (Lowell Press), as well as the recipient of the 1965 E. P. Dutton award for Best Sports Stories.

When asked how he had happened to select quarterbacks as a subject, Mr. Anderson replied: "The quarterback really makes the game. Whenever a play is started, it's the quarterback who has the ball. He's a different breed from the other players. They look to him for leadership."

Mr. Anderson lives in Tenafly, New Jersey, with his wife and four children.

Index

177

Index

178

Index

Index

Index

Index